The Music Library

The History of Country Music

by Stuart A. Kallen

LUCENT
BOOKS®

THOMSON

GALE

San Diego • Detroit • New York • San Francisco • Cleveland • New Haven, Conn. • Waterville, Maine • London • Munich

T████████N

GALE

© 2003 by Lucent Books. Lucent Books is an imprint of The Gale Group, Inc.,
a division of Thomson Learning, Inc.

Lucent Books® and Thomson Learning™ are trademarks used herein under license.

For more information, contact
Lucent Books
27500 Drake Rd.
Farmington Hills, MI 48331-3535
Or you can visit our Internet site at http://www.gale.com

LIBRARY OF CONGRESS CATALOGING-IN-PUBLICATION DATA

Kallen, Stuart A., 1955–
    The History of country music / by Stuart A. Kallen.
p. cm. — (The music library)
Summary: A history of country music that discusses its roots, influences, and various
types including bluegrass, honky-tonk, cowboy music, western swing, and rockabilly.
Includes bibliographical references (p.).
    ISBN 1-59018-124-7 (alk. paper)
    1. Country music—History and criticism—Juvenile literature. [1. Country music.]
I. Title. II. Music library (San Diego, Calif.)
    ML3524 .K35 2003
    781.642'09—dc21
                                                                2002000664

Printed in the United States of America

• Contents •

• Foreword •

In the nineteenth century English novelist Charles Kingsley wrote, "Music speaks straight to our hearts and spirits, to the very core and root of our souls. . . . Music soothes us, stirs us up . . . melts us to tears." As Kingsley stated, music is much more than just a pleasant arrangement of sounds. It is the resonance of emotion, a joyful noise, a human endeavor that can soothe the spirit or excite the soul. Musicians can also imitate the expressive palate of the earth, from the violent fury of a hurricane to the gentle flow of a babbling brook.

The word music is derived from the fabled Greek muses, the children of Apollo who ruled the realms of inspiration and imagination. Composers have long called upon the muses for help and insight. Music is not merely the result of emotions and pleasurable sensations, however.

Music is a discipline subject to formal study and analysis. It involves the juxtaposition of creative elements such as rhythm, melody, and harmony with intellectual aspects of composition, theory, and instrumentation. Like painters

mixing red, blue, and yellow into thousands of colors, musicians blend these various elements to create classical symphonies, jazz improvisations, country ballads, and rock-and-roll tunes.

Throughout centuries of musical history, individual musical elements have been blended and modified in infinite ways. The resulting sounds may convey a whole range of moods, emotions, reactions, and messages. Music, then, is both an expression and reflection of human experience and emotion.

The foundations of modern musical styles were laid down by the first ancient musicians who used wood, rocks, animal skins—and their own bodies—to re-create the sounds of the natural world in which they lived. With their hands, their feet, and their very breath they ignited the passions of listeners and moved them to their feet. The dancing, in turn, had a mesmerizing and hypnotic effect that allowed people to transcend their worldly concerns. Through music they could achieve a level of shared experience that could not be found in other forms of communication. For this reason, music has always been part of religious endeavors, from ancient Egyptian religious ceremonies to modern Christian masses. And it has inspired dance movements from kings and queens spinning the minuet to punk rockers slamming together in a mosh pit.

By examining musical genres ranging from Western classical music to rock and roll, readers will find a new understanding of old music and develop an appreciation for new sounds. Books in Lucent's Music Library focus on the music, the musicians, the instruments, and on music's place in cultural history. The songs and artists examined may be easily found in the CD and sheet music collections of local libraries so that readers may study and enjoy the music covered in the books. Informative sidebars, annotated bibliographies, and complete indexes highlight the text in each volume and provide young readers with many opportunities for further discussion and research.

Introduction

American Roots Music

The term "country music" is generally used today to describe the music played on country radio stations and in videos shown on country music television channels. The videos feature handsome men and pretty women dressed in tight jeans, cowboy boots, and other western gear. They dance and sing about love, heartbreak, God, and the U.S.A. while playing guitars, mandolins, banjos, fiddles, and pedal steel guitars.

While the slick sounds of modern country artists sell millions of CDs, country music superstars from Garth Brooks to the Dixie Chicks find their inspiration in the past. And the roots of country may be traced back several generations to the 1920s to include the sweet gospel-tinged harmonies of the Carter Family, the hot mandolin picking of bluegrass founder Bill Monroe, the polished violin arrangements of the king of western swing Bob Wills, and the sad lonesome ballads of Hank Williams. These musicians of the past,

and dozens of others, were the country superstars in their day and continue to profoundly influence the musical style today.

The Music of Appalachia

Modern country was born in the southern Appalachian Mountains, the green rolling hills that dominate the American countryside in parts of the Carolinas, Virginia, West Virginia, Kentucky, and Tennessee. The area was first settled in the mid-1700s by English and Scotch-Irish immigrants who brought with them fiddles, guitars, mandolins, and other easy-to-carry instruments. Although the rocky, hilly terrain did not make the best farmland, the families were self-sufficient, hunting and growing enough food to survive. Money was scarce, but people made or bartered for what they needed, and few people had "store-bought" items.

Although the U.S. population grew during the nineteenth century, the Appalachians were inaccessible to all but the most determined travelers, and the descendants of the first settlers remained extremely isolated. With little in the way of outside entertainment, almost everybody sang and played an instrument. Music based on ancient English and Irish song was popular, and vocal church music, sung in groups with no instrumental accompaniment, was also a very important part of life.

At the beginning of the twentieth century, the modern world rapidly encroached on the Appalachian people. Railroads, coal mines, and factories were built, and the people who formerly lived by subsistence agriculture began moving into the "dollar economy," where they could buy newly available cars, radios, electric appliances, and records. Men and women who formerly spent their days hunting, fishing, and making necessary goods started to dig in coal mines, punch factory clocks, and work on the railroad.

These changes brought new influences into the traditional music of Appalachia. People began to sing about

Hank Williams is one of many artists who had a major influence on country music.

Artists like Garth Brooks have brought country music a long way from its early American roots.

their common problems, such as loneliness far from home, broken relationships, working for low wages, living in poverty, and the strength found in religion.

A Healing Tonic

The introduction of radio and the record player also brought changes to country songs. The music of African American blues and gospel, Louisiana Cajun, western cowboy, and even jazz formed a rich cultural stew as the songs of Appalachia spread across the southern and western United States. Although the style was still derided in big

cities as hillbilly music, it was, in fact, true American roots music, influenced not by European classical composers, but by field hands, farmers, and millions of other working women and men.

Today country music is divided into categories, which emerged virtually simultaneously while drawing from various influences. These styles include bluegrass, western swing, honky-tonk, rockabilly, the Nashville Sound, and new country. The lyrics have remained important, while the musical changes generally rely on the simple three-chord patterns also basic to rock and blues. Instrumental virtuosity, however, is important, and some of the hottest "licks" can be heard coming from the players of country fiddles, guitars, pedal steels, mandolins, and banjos.

In the twenty-first century country music has grown into a big business. The Dixie Chicks have won armloads of Grammy Awards, and Garth Brooks is the best-selling solo act in music history—bigger than Elvis Presley, Michael Jackson, and other rock stars. While the players have grown rich, the aim of the music has changed little since its early incarnations in the Blue Ridge and Great Smoky Mountains. Country music is and was a healing tonic for anyone with a broken heart, the lonesome blues, or just a basic need to get up and dance the night away.

Chapter One

The Early Years of Country

Country music is, first and foremost, American music, and its story begins with the founding of the country itself. From the moment the first English settlers came to the New World, they were singing and playing songs that dated to sixteenth-century England, Ireland, and Scotland. Even as America grew over the years, only 10 percent of the people lived in cities. The rest lived in isolated agricultural communities where little had changed. With strong cultural, financial, and political ties to Great Britain, the songs of Americans were based on British music. As Charles K. Wolfe writes in *The Illustrated History of Country Music:*

> The core of these songs was brought over by the first settlers, and the songs range in age from medieval times to the days immediately before the ships sailed for the New World. Since the Middle Ages there had been a thriving

folk-song culture among English peasants and urban poor, and since these people were illiterate, the songs had been passed on orally from generation to generation. This process continued to function with little interruption once the settlers had established themselves in America; the songs were of love, death, trauma, and infamy, and in those days of slow change they lost none of their appeal from generation to generation. They enabled the singers and listeners to see the world in very personal terms. [1]

Making Songs American

Since the songs were not written down in books, and few people could read in any case, the lyrics of these songs changed over time to fit in with American experiences and culture. For example, the Irish song "Canaday-i-o" about migrating to Canada was transformed into a tale of lumberjacks called

"The Backwoodsmen" when sung in the north woods. Later as people migrated west, the melody remained the same, but the lyrics were changed once again as the lumberjacks became bison hunters in "Buffalo Skinners." In *Old as the Hills,* Steven D. Price describes how songs evolved over time:

> Names of characters and locales were Americanized: "The Oxford Girl" became "The Knoxville Girl," while "Bonnie George Campbell" turned into "Georgie Collins." Titles of nobility bit the dust: "Lord Randal" found him-self in some parts of America as "Jimmy Randal," "Sir Lionel" be-came "Old Bangum." As British English became 'American' hill-country vernacular, the British version of "The Three Ravens"—*There were three ravens sat on a tree . . . And they were black as black as might be . . .* lost a bird somewhere between Scotland and Kentucky: *Two old crows sat on a tree . . . Black and ugly as they could be.* [2]

The old songs were affected by the American temperament as well. Long

A fiddle accompanies a group of early American settlers traveling by covered wagon.

British ballads—that is, songs that told stories—were drastically shortened by pioneers, who seemed to have little time for songs such as the thirty-five-verse "The Lass of Loch Royal," which morphed into the three-verse "Who's Gonna Shoe Your Pretty Little Foot?" In addition, Americans added over-wrought emotion and sentimentality to British songs that had originally been sung with what Wolfe describes as "a cold, detached, impersonal air."[3]

The expressive emotional feeling was coupled with the American interpretation of morality. While British folk songs often had graphic—and humorous—descriptions of sexual relations, Americans quickly dropped these lyrics. Americans, however, were quite tolerant of violence, especially between lovers. In "Pretty Polly," based on the British "The Gosport Tragedy," a man murders his girlfriend because he doesn't want to marry her after making her pregnant. In "Pearl Bryan," two men murder a girl and cut off her head. As Price writes: "Victims were shot, stabbed, drowned, poisoned, or otherwise done in."[4] American morals demanded, however, that songs attach stern warnings to such bloody tales. For example, "Pearl Bryan" ends with

Young ladies, now take warning;
young men are so unjust;
It may be your best lover, but you
know not whom to trust.
Pearl died away from home and
friends, out on that lonely spot;
Take heed! Take heed! Believe me,
girls; don't let this be your lot.[5]

Religious Roots

The warnings attached to love ballads were called for at a time when religion played a central role in the lives of country people. Sedate British hymns, some dating back to the tenth century, were deemed inadequate for the exuberant religious revivals that periodically swept across the country. As hundreds of people gathered in backwoods churches, they turned to songbooks such as *The Southern Harmony*, published in 1835, which contained more than three hundred Americanized religious songs.

Again, folk melodies served as a basis for new words more appropriate for the American experience. Songbooks published by singer Ira Sankey and evangelist Dwight L. Moody in the late nineteenth century contained songs such as "When the Roll Is Called Up Yonder," "The Drunkard's Lone Child," and "Life's Railway to Heaven" that had a decidedly American take on salvation. And these books were popular—the Sankey-Moody books sold more than 50 million copies between 1875 and 1908.

These songs were often sung by quartets who perfected four-part harmony that would later become standard in country music. In fact, many of the first nationally popular country music stars began their musical careers singing in gospel choirs.

The Wandering Minstrels

Publishers hired talented quartets to travel the country, singing their songs—and selling their songbooks—in

Early country songs were performed by quartets of talented musicians known as wandering minstrels.

churches throughout the South. Meanwhile, other entertainers carried Americanized versions of ancient British ballads on the road. These people played in taverns, minstrel shows, medicine shows, vaudeville theaters, and even steamboat dining rooms. Some of the songs played by wandering musicians—such as "Blue Tail Fly," "Old Dan Tucker," and "Buffalo Gals, Won't You Come Out Tonight?"—became national "hits" after they were published on sheet music. Wolfe writes about the fiddle-tune standard "Turkey in the Straw": "The song might well have been a folk melody before it was published (there were similar tunes in both Irish and English folk music), but its publication and subsequent performance in hundreds of minstrel

The Medicine Show

In The Illustrated History of Country Music, *Charles K. Wolfe describes the southern medicine show:*

The medicine show consisted of three or four people who would pull their wagon or truck into small towns, give free "entertainment" to attract a crowd, and try to sell various medicines and elixirs of somewhat dubious quality. The shows usually contained all the elements of a larger minstrel show: songs, jokes, skits, and even the burlesque drama. . . . Clayton McMichen, a member of the famous Skillet Lickers and national champion fiddler, recalled . . . his experiences with such medicine shows:

> I worked in medicine shows as late as 1936. I rebuilt me a Dodge Northeast generator of 1,000 watts. Bought a little motor for lights and loudspeaker. We called the medicine shows "the kerosene circuit" or "the physic operas." People had tired feet and you had to be funny. . . .

> I was raised on one password: "Sold Out, Doc." The medicine to fight neuralgia and rheumatism cost $1.00 a bottle and we really sold it. We took in $300 or $400, traveled in a Model T, carried a hammer and saw to build a platform. Before and after World War I, Tennessee was thicker with physic operas than Georgia. . . .

The type of medicine sold in the shows, of course, varied from doctor to doctor, from show to show. Many of today's country musicians did their stints in medicine shows, and they tell hair-raising tales of what went into the medicines. Some were made up of just colored water, and some mountain shows actually used complex concoctions of herbs as the elixir, but [*Grand Ole Opry*] pioneer Kirk McGee recalls getting tangled up with a dope-sniffing doctor who used plain old gasoline as the base for his cure-all. The grass-roots medicine shows lingered on into the 1950s.

shows across the country certainly helped establish it as an anthem of rural America."[6]

Sheet music played the same role as records and CDs did in a later era, and some popular songs could sell as many as 1 million pieces of sheet music. In 1910 alone, more than 2 billion copies of sheet music were sold in North America. Amateur and professional musicians would learn songs from the written music and play them at parties, barn dances, and local entertainment venues.

While musicians played pianos, guitars, banjos, mandolins, and other instruments, violins—light, easy to carry, and cheap to repair—were especially popular. Nearly every social gathering in the South required a fiddler to entertain the crowd. Fiddlers played when neighbors gathered to raise a barn, harvest a crop, or celebrate a milestone. And as Robert K. Oermann writes in *A Century of Country,* the fiddling tradition "is as old as the nation. Thomas Jefferson and Davy Crockett were both country fiddlers. Confederate soldiers took their fiddles to campgrounds and were often photographed with them."[7]

The fiddle was the instrument of choice among Civil War soldiers because it was both portable and inexpensive.

To have a party, people cleared the furniture from their cabins to make way for dancers. Fiddlers were also the center of attention at barn dances, which usually lasted from dusk until dawn. In Texas, where people had to travel greater distances to get together, barn dances could last up to three days.

Fiddlers were called upon to play dozens of tunes, often based on Irish jigs and English reels, sometimes playing solo, sometimes in groups. And as top-selling country fiddler Clinton Gregory recalls, many of the fiddlers had been taught by their relatives:

> I learned to play the fiddle from my father . . . who was a champion fiddler back in Virginia. His dad was a fiddler, and *his* dad. It goes back five generations. Playing square dances when I was a kid is basically how I learned to play. The three main ingredients for a professional square dance is plenty of bootleg whiskey to drink, plenty of food, and good music. [8]

Because Gregory's father was a champion fiddler, he must have won fiddle contests where dozens of men (and in recent times, women) compete for prizes or, more important, for the title of the best fiddler in the county or state. Fiddling contests were held independent of barn dances, and such events, held at local schoolhouses or county fairs, could attract thousands of people from miles around.

Guitars and Banjos

While the fiddler and his bow ruled the southern barn dance, by the end of the nineteenth century, there were plenty of guitar players around. And guitar players had been singing songs of love, death, work, and joy as far back as sixteenth-century Europe.

While guitars were expensive and rare in the hills of Appalachia, by the 1890s several companies began to manufacture inexpensive guitars. Even rural musicians in isolated regions could order them from the Sears Catalog, along with instruction and music books, and have them delivered to their nearest post office or railway depot. And the instruments were cheap—of the seven guitars in the 1894 Sears Catalog, the least expensive was two dollars.

In 1902 the Gibson Company of Kalamazoo, Michigan, began making higher-quality guitars and mandolins, and it sent string orchestras into the countryside to drum up business for its instruments, which the company labeled the "Musical Pals of the Nation." [9]

Rural guitar players were often influenced by African American musicians who played blues, ragtime, and gospel songs. Black musicians also played banjos, instruments with roots in ancient Africa. By the late nineteenth century, rural whites had adapted the banjo to their musical styles, and combined with fiddles, guitars, and mandolins, the basic instruments of twentieth-century country music were in place.

Hillbilly Music

While stringed instruments were "old as the hills," in 1877 a mechanical invention took country music beyond its rural roots to millions of eager listeners throughout the world.

When Thomas Edison invented the phonograph, he thought it might be useful for dictation in a business setting. No one thought of selling music for the machine, which later became known as a "record player," until 1891 when Columbia Records printed a catalog to sell wax cylinders featuring hits such as "The Esquimaux 'Eskimo' Dance," a clarinet solo backed by barking dogs and a hammer striking an anvil.

People were eager to hear these primitive offerings, however, and the record business quickly kicked into high gear. By 1895 Columbia was selling hundreds of cylinders a day, and by 1900 the company was offering more than five thousand selections. By that time, the flat record had been perfected and ten-inch discs sold for as little as a dollar.

By the early 1900s, there were dozens of record labels releasing everything from President McKinley's inauguration speech to minstrels, bagpipes, and comic songs. The forerunners to country music were also recorded. Between 1904 and 1912, men such as Cal Stewart, Billy Murray, and Billy Golden released humorous songs by characters referred to as "country bumpkins" or "rubes." This style was called "lowbrow" as opposed to "highbrow," which included classical music and opera.

The catalogs released by the record companies described each offering. The 1901 listing of the country classic "Arkansas Traveler" is "a native sitting in front of his hut scraping his fiddle, and answering the interruptions of the stranger with witty sallies [quips]." [10]

Around the same time, these rubes, or unsophisticated country fellows, were first referred to as hillbillies. In 1900 a reporter for the *New York Journal* attended a southern square dance and described the people he saw, writing: "A Hill-Billie is a free and untrammeled white citizen of Alabama, who lives in the hills, has no 'job' to speak of, dresses as he can, talks as he pleases, drinks whiskey when he can get it, and fires off his revolver as the fancy takes him." [11] Before long this description replaced bumpkin or rube to describe almost any rural southerner.

In 1922 a few hillbillies who happened to be in New York City walked into the offices of Victor Records unannounced and declared that they were ready to record some music. Fiddlers Eck Robertson and Henry Gilliland were dressed as cowboys and had just come from a Civil War veterans reunion in Richmond, Virginia, where they turned a hotel meeting room into a barn dance. The two musicians impressed the Victor executives enough that within weeks the company released the first "hillbilly" record—the lightning-fast fiddle tune "Sallie Gooden" backed by "Arkansas Traveler."

Although they had to compete with other new forms of recorded music, such as jazz, blues, and swing, the hill-billy records charted respectable sales numbers. In 1922 "Wreck on the Southern Old 97," written by former mill hand Henry Whitter about a 1903 train accident, sold a million copies. That same year the hillbilly tune "It Ain't Gonna Rain No Mo'" by Wendell Hall sold a phenomenal 2 million copies. Hillbilly music was topping the charts and in 1922 alone helped push record sales figures over $105 million.

With the astonishing success of hill-billy music, New York talent scouts began combing the South for performers. In the summer of 1927, Victor Records sent Ralph Peer to Bristol, Virginia—in the heart of Appalachia—where he managed to audition a dizzying variety of gospel singers, string bands, balladeers, and others in a twelve-day marathon. Two of those acts signed, Jimmie Rodgers and the Carter Family, quickly became legends of country music.

The Carter Family, from the appropriately named Poor Valley, Virginia,

A group of girls listen to an early phonograph, an invention that revolutionized the music industry.

The Carter Family, from left to right, Maybelle, Alvin P., and his wife, Sara. The trio emphasized vocal arrangements in their music.

consisted of Alvin P. Carter (known as A.P.), his wife, Sara, and his sister-in-law Maybelle. This innovative trio utilized soaring three-part harmonies, shifting the focus of country music to sweet-sounding vocal arrangements, an area that had achieved scant attention by earlier hillbilly singers. A.P. was a musicologist who unearthed or wrote most of the group's material, along with Maybelle and Sara. These songs—including "Wildwood Flower," "I'm Thinking Tonight of My Blue Eyes," "Will the Circle Be Unbroken,"

"Hello Stranger," and others—are considered country standards today and have been covered by almost everybody in the business. Sara was the first female country music star, and Maybelle's thumb picking, later known as "Carter Picking," made the guitar a lead instrument for the first time on record. Although the Carter family disbanded in the early 1940s, their music influenced a generation of country and rock musicians in the decades that followed.

Turn Your Radio On

The success of hillbilly music inspired record companies to sign hundreds of other hillbilly artists. Coincidentally, another new form of mass communication came along that topped records in its ability to reach the masses.

The first commercial radio station went on the air in 1920, and by the end of 1923 there were more than 550 broadcasting stations in the United States. Since there was no national programming, stations scrambled to fill hours of airtime with local entertainment. In the South this was an open invitation to country music performers, some of whom, such as Eddy Arnold, were recruited by agents while playing music on their front porches.

This new medium was so popular that a national poll showed that people would sooner give up their telephones, refrigerators, and even their beds, rather than their trusty radios. As country superstar Charley Pride says, "The radio was my only way of finding out what

Jimmie Rodgers—the Singing Brakeman

Country music is often about trains, travel, being broke, and singing the blues, and Jimmie Rodgers started it all. Rollin stone.com, the website of Rolling Stone *magazine published this biography of the legendary "Singing Brakeman":*

His brass plaque in the Country Music Hall of Fame reads, "Jimmie Rodgers name stands foremost in the country music field as the man who started it all." This is a fair assessment. The "Singing Brakeman" and the "Mississippi Blue Yodeler," whose six-year career was cut short by tuberculosis, became the first nationally known star of country music and the direct influence of many later performers. . . . [Born and raised in Meridian, Mississippi,] Rodgers sang about rounders and gamblers, bounders and ramblers—and he knew what he sang about. At age 14 he went to work as a railroad brakeman, and on the rails he stayed until a pulmonary hemorrhage sidetracked him to the medicine show circuit in 1925. The years with the trains harmed his health but helped his music. In an era when Rodgers' contemporaries were singing only mountain and mountain/folk music, he fused hillbilly country, gospel, jazz, blues, pop, cowboy, and folk; and many of his best songs were his compositions, including . . . ["Waiting for a Train,"] ["Travelin' Blues,"] ["Train Whistle Blues,"] ["Blue Yodel No. 1,"] and ["T for Texas,"] and his thirteen blue yodels. . . . His instrumental accompaniment consisted sometimes of his guitar only, while at other times a full jazz band (horns and all) backed him up. Country fans could have asked for no better hero/star—someone who thought what they thought, felt what they felt, and sang about the common person honestly and beautifully.

Legendary country musician, Jimmie Rodgers.

was out there beyond the cotton fields of home."[12]

People were buying radios at an incredible rate, and by the mid-1920s tens of millions of Americans had purchased "Radiolas" for around seventy-five dollars—a dizzying sum in an era when a new Model T Ford cost little more than four hundred dollars.

In Dallas, Atlanta, and other southern cities, live hillbilly acts attracted thousands of listeners. And country records were played over the airwaves for the first time. Some of these early artists—including Uncle Dave Macon, Gid Tanner and His Skillet Lickers,

A woman listens to an early radio. Thousands of listeners in the 1920s tuned in to hear country music.

and country superstar Hank Williams—went on to become household names in the South.

By 1924 listeners across the country could tune in on Saturday nights to the powerful 50,000-watt WLS in Chicago to hear the *National Barn Dance.* This wildly popular show featured romantic country crooners, foot-tapping string bands, yodeling cowboys, cornball comics, and even barbershop quartets singing slick four-part harmonies. In 1932 the show was picked up by NBC and broadcast on thirty stations from coast to coast. The show made national stars out of regular performers such as Bradley Kincaid, Grandpa Jones, and cowgirl singer Patsy Montana—the first female country star to sell a million records.

In 1949 ABC began televising thirty-nine weekly episodes a year, and each show featured nearly a hundred performers. Before it was canceled in the early 1960s, the *National Barn Dance* had been delivering the best in country music to a national audience for more than forty years.

Grand Ole Opry Every Saturday Night

The success of the *National Barn Dance* inspired the creation of dozens of similar shows throughout the country, and none was more popular—or enduring—than the *Grand Ole Opry* on WSM in Nashville, Tennessee. When the show went on the air on December 26, 1925, people were able to hear it across a wide region because of

A large crowd attends a performance of the Grand Ole Opry.

WSM's powerful 5,000-watt signal. The show, however, did not receive its name until 1927 when after a formal program of highbrow opera, music announcer George D. Hays came on the air and said, "For the past hour we have been listening to music taken largely from the Grand Opera, but from now on we will present *The Grand Ole Opry.*"[13]

By the end of the 1930s, the star of the *Opry* was Roy Acuff, "the King of Country Music." Acuff's band, the Smoky Mountain Boys, was the first to feature a Dobro, that is, a slide guitar with a metal resonator in the middle. Acuff was a hard-charging fiddle player and singer who wrote about his singing style: "I rared back like I was going after the cows, the same way when I used to drive the cows out to pasture on the farm. In them hills up there . . . I sang loud."[14] Acuff's hits—such as "The Great Speckled Bird," "Wabash Cannonball," "Wreck on the Highway," and "I Saw the Light"—became instant country standards.

The *Opry* was broadcast every Saturday night from the Ryman Auditorium, and playing there became the goal of every aspiring country musician. Some who passed the audition—such as Loretta Lynn, Hank Williams, Kitty Wells, and Dolly Parton—went on to become major country stars.

Soothing the Soul

The advent of programs like the *Grand Ole Opry* shook traditional music to its very roots, inspiring thousands of country musicians throughout the South. Practically overnight the old-time music found a national audience eager to hear "She'll Be Comin' 'Round the Mountain," "Buffalo Gals," "Mountain Dew," "You Are My Sunshine," "Wildwood Flower," and thousands of other songs based on centuries-old British folk tunes. But even as the same old songs were played, the music itself began to evolve. Fiddle licks got faster, harmonies tighter, and the creative energies of a new generation of artists began to shape and mold the music to fit a new era. Although the twentieth century was scarred by wars, the Great Depression, and unrest, the music of the hills continued to soothe the souls of Americans wherever they were on Saturday night.

Chapter Two

The Sounds of Bluegrass

From its inception, country was string band music, featuring guitars, fiddles, banjos, mandolins, and the thumping stand-up bass. The fastest fiddlers were widely respected and honored with prizes in fiddle contests throughout the South. By the 1920s, however, country music had absorbed a wide variety of influences from ragtime to blues and jazz, and a new sound, later dubbed bluegrass, emerged.

Bluegrass depends on lightning-fast cascades of notes that are not written down on sheet music but made up by the player on the spot, a process called improvisation. There are usually no electric instruments involved, and the two-, three-, and four-part vocals rely on high-pitched, sometimes raucous harmonies. A standard bluegrass band consists of five pieces—violin, mandolin, guitar, banjo, and stand-up bass—with other instruments, such as a harmonica or Dobro occasionally added to the mix.

Although bluegrass sounds as old as the hills, it did not evolve into its present style until the mid-1940s. But it began with the success of barn dance radio shows, such as the *Grand Ole Opry*, in the 1920s and '30s. Successful radio performers with their banjos, fiddles, guitars, and mandolins lured thousands of musicians out of the hills, and many of them came from families where "hot pickin'" was a way of life dating back generations. In fact, some of the most popular groups that served as a prototype for bluegrass were brothers who played guitar-mandolin duets. For example, the Allen Brothers from Chattanooga, Tennessee, had a major hit with "Salty Dog Blues" in 1927. The Callahan Brothers had one of the biggest hits of the 1930s with "My Curly Headed Baby," and the Dixon Brothers had a major hit with Roy Acuff's song "Wreck on the Highway." These brother acts, along with many other family duets, featured tight two-part vocals, with one voice singing the

Country Jazz

John and Alan Lomax were a father-son team of "ballad hunters" who scoured the hills, back roads, and even prisons of rural America in the early twentieth century recording the pure, traditional sounds of poor country musicians. Along the way, they discovered soon-to-be folk standards such as "Rock Island Line," "John Henry," and "Midnight Special" while promoting the careers of the then unknown Woody Guthrie and Huddie "Leadbelly" Ledbetter. In 1959, during the height of the folk revival he helped spawn, Alan Lomax compared the bluegrass of Bill Monroe to improvised jazz music. His Esquire *magazine article was reprinted in* The Bill Monroe Reader, *edited by Tom Ewing. Lomax wrote:*

[T]he] freshest sound comes from the so-called Bluegrass band—a sort of mountain Dixieland combo in which the five-string banjo, America's only indigenous folk instrument, carries the lead like a hot clarinet. The mandolin plays bursts reminiscent of jazz trumpet choruses; a heavily bowed fiddle supplies trombone-like hoedown solos; while a framed guitar and slapped bass make up the rhythm section. Everything goes at top volume, with harmonized choruses behind a lead singer who hollers in the high, lonesome style beloved in the American backwoods. The result is folk music in overdrive with a silvery, rippling, pinging sound.

melody and the other singing a high falsetto harmony above the tenor range. In the background, speedy guitar and mandolin licks filled in breaks between the singing with flowing torrents of notes.

The Father of Bluegrass

In 1927 Birch, Charlie, and Bill Monroe, a trio of brothers from Kentucky, made their first appearance on the country circuit. Billed as the Monroe Brothers, these men were proficient on several instruments, but Bill settled on the mandolin, Charlie on guitar, and Birch on fiddle.

Like many others raised in rural hills, the Monroes were very poor but were surrounded by music as children. Their mother was an old-time fiddle player, and her brother Pendleton—later immortalized by Bill in the song "Uncle Pen"—also played the fiddle. Their father had a high-pitched tenor voice, and his brother sang a harmony even higher above that. In addition to their family jam sessions, the Monroe Brothers were inspired by an African American musician, Arnold Schultz, whom they often heard playing guitar and fiddle at country dances in their hometown of Rosine.

In the late '20s the Monroes left the poverty of Kentucky to work in a Chicago oil refinery washing out oil barrels with gasoline. For respite from this toxic work, they journeyed to the radio station WLS, where they managed to work as part-time dancers for the *National Barn Dance* radio show. The trio also landed work playing music in the Midwest, but Birch quit when he decided there was no future in it. Charlie and Bill carried on, playing throughout the Midwest and South.

Capitalizing on Bill's ability to play virtuoso mandolin licks at a blistering speed, the Monroe Brothers attracted a devoted audience. And they did not go unnoticed by record executives—the brothers recorded sixty gospel and folk songs for RCA between 1936 and 1938. These records quickly climbed the country charts in the South, outselling nearly all the other brother acts.

Although the group was popular, Bill was restless, wanting a large string band to play the music he heard in his head. Since the brothers were not getting along anyway, they went their separate ways in 1938. In 1939 Bill put together a four-piece band, playing mandolin with a guitarist, fiddler, and bassist. To honor Kentucky, known as the Bluegrass State, Monroe called his band the Blue Grass Boys.

In September 1939 Monroe's band landed a coveted spot on the *Grand Ole Opry.* The Blue Grass Boys were the first quartet to perform at the *Opry,* and the lively music of the string band enlivened the audience. But it was more than the hot picking that mesmerized the audience. Monroe had a unique singing style, described by *Opry* host George D. Hays: "There is that authentic wail in his high-pitched voice that one hears in the evening in the country when Mother Nature sighs and retires for the night." Monroe himself described it as "the high, lonesome sound." [15]

Bill (left) and Charlie Monroe. Bill later went on to develop the bluegrass style of country music.

Life as a Blue Grass Boy

Bill Monroe's Blue Grass Boys were extremely popular in the late 1940s, but life on the road was tough on the musicians, as Earl Scruggs writes on the "Biography of Earl Scruggs" website:

We were working all the time. Sometimes we wouldn't see a bed from one end of the week 'til the other. In theaters, we would do four or five or six shows a day from eleven in the morning until eleven at night. . . .

It was a must then to make it back to the Opry on Saturday night. Sometimes, if we were over on the East Coast somewhere, it was all we could do to make it back. But the Opry meant so much to the people then in the towns. . . .

It was hard traveling then on bad roads in a stretched-out car with no place to lie down. Sometimes you'd feel so bad and fall asleep and then wake up and someone would maybe tell a story and we'd laugh and feel good again. But Bill would never let the music go down no matter how tired we were. If a man would slack off, he would move over and get that mandolin close up on him and get him back up there. He would shove you and you would shove him and you would really get on it.

We played in rain, we played in snow, we played where the power would go off and we would have to play by lantern light with no sound. We had two bad wrecks, but nobody got hurt. The way we had to drive to make dates, it's a wonder we weren't killed. But we made it, and it toughened you up to encounter and overcome these difficulties. It seemed to make Bill stronger and it brought out the deep feeling and love he had for what he was doing.

"Play It Good and Clean"

Although the Blue Grass Boys were extremely popular, touring widely and playing at state fairs, baseball games, and tent shows, the restless Monroe was still not satisfied. The band's sound was too similar to dozens of other string bands recording at the time.

In 1945 the mandolin picker was finally able to put together the sound that would become synonymous with his name. After hiring guitarist Lester Flatt, three-finger-style banjo picker Earl Scruggs, fiddler Chubby Wise, and bassist Howard "Cedric Rainwater" Watts, the new Blue Grass Boys burned up the stage at the *Opry*. As bluegrass musician John Hartford says, "Bluegrass music had a passion and a ferociousness that really got you excited. . . . [E]very note was just as clear as crystal." [16]

In the years before it was routine for rock stars to receive hysterical adulation from fans, the Blue Grass Boys were a country music phenomenon. The audience screamed and yelled when they played their bluegrass "breakdowns" (songs played in double time). On tour the band broke attendance records wherever they went. Young musicians played the band's 78 RPM records on slower speeds on their record players desperately trying to imitate the red-hot picking licks of Monroe and the others. And groups across the South combed the woods for banjo and mandolin players so they could imitate the bluegrass sound. By 1953 folklorist Mike Seeger estimated that every southern town with a population over a thousand had at least one amateur bluegrass band.

Today Monroe's songs—"Blue Moon of Kentucky," "Uncle Pen," "In the Pines," "Molly & Tenbrooks," "My Sweet Blue-Eyed Darlin'," and others—are bluegrass standards beloved by musicians and fans. As to the secret of his success, Monroe stated plainly: "You always play it the best way you can. . . . Play it good and clean and play good melodies with it, but keep perfect time. It takes really good timing with bluegrass music, and it takes some good high voices to really deliver it right." [17]

In October 1989 Monroe celebrated his fiftieth year at the *Opry,* and the

A 1982 picture of Bill Monroe and his band the Blue Grass Boys. Monroe played music for more than fifty years.

seventy-eight-year-old mandolin player sang and played as quick as he always had. In 1996 "the Father of Bluegrass Music" died just a few days short of his eighty-fifth birthday. The fifteen hundred guests who attended his funeral were a who's who of country music superstars. Those who delivered eulogies included Marty Stuart, Vince Gill, Ricky Skaggs, Alison Krauss, and Patty Loveless.

"Foggy Mountain Breakdown"

By the time of his death, Monroe had seen his unique music style adapted by countless players from Nashville to Europe, Asia, and beyond. And the reach of bluegrass was extended by some of the 175 musicians who played with Monroe over the years.

The first of Monroe's players to move on and create their own sound were Flatt, Scruggs, and Watts, who quit the Blue Grass Boys in 1948 to form the Foggy Mountain Boys. In his few, short years with Monroe, Scruggs had quickly become a star in his own right, as Bob Artis writes in *Bluegrass:* "Audiences just couldn't believe that anyone could play the banjo like Earl Scruggs. It was so fast and smooth, and

Lester Flatt (left) and Earl Scruggs left Bill Monroe's Bluegrass Boys to form The Foggy Mountain Boys in 1948

there were so many notes, but all the melody and everything else was right there in the shower of banjo music. The crowds would roar every time Earl stepped to the microphone."[18] Much of the thrill was the sound of the greased-lightning, three-finger picking style that Scruggs had perfected since he had begun playing the banjo in North Carolina at the age of four. After leaving the Blue Grass Boys, Scruggs wrote "Foggy Mountain Breakdown," a song that became an instant classic as part of every banjo player's repertoire.

In the mid-1950s the Foggy Mountain Boys hired Buck Graves to play the Dobro, a guitar with what appears to be a metal hubcap attached to the face of the instrument. This metal resonator makes the Dobro louder than an average guitar, something that could compete with Scruggs's ringing banjo. Using a steel bar slide-guitar style, Graves "turned the dobro into a powerful lead voice, slipping and swooping like a barnstorming plane,"[19] as Steven D. Price writes in *Old as the Hills*. And just as Scruggs had breathed new life into the banjo, Graves permanently elevated the Dobro to exalted status in the world of bluegrass.

By the late 1950s the Foggy Mountain Boys were taking their brand of blistering bluegrass breakdowns beyond the traditional country circuit to college campuses and folk festivals, where a new generation was eager to hear their sound. In 1962, when Scruggs wrote "The Ballad of Jed Clampett," the theme song for the TV comedy *The Beverly Hillbillies,* the

Earl Scruggs and his sons formed the 1970's band, The Earl Scruggs Revue.

group Flatt & Scruggs became a household name because of their many appearances on the extremely popular show. And in 1967 "Foggy Mountain Breakdown" was used as the theme song for the hit movie *Bonnie & Clyde.*

Although Flatt & Scruggs broke up in 1969, the king of bluegrass banjo continued to make innovative music, as Robert Oermann writes in *A Century of Country:*

> Scruggs formed a group with his sons that explored country's connections to rock, jazz, folk, and pop. The Earl Scruggs Revue toured and recorded with everyone from Bob Dylan and Joan Baez to The Byrds. . . . In 1971 Scruggs was instrumental in wedding the folkrock of The Nitty

Gritty Dirt Band with a who's who of old-time country music on the band's landmark [album] *Will the Circle Be Unbroken.* Among the participants were Roy Acuff, Maybelle Carter, Merle Travis, Doc Watson, Brother Oswald, and Norman Blake. [20]

Bands of Brothers

While Flatt & Scruggs helped spread the popularity of bluegrass to a wide audience, several others made their mark in the world of country music. The Stanley Brothers, Carter and Ralph, began playing after World War II. In 1947 they had a hit with "Little Glass of Wine," a cross between the old-time mountain music style and bluegrass, with relaxed two-part harmonies backed by a frenetic guitar and banjo.

Carter's rich "high and lonesome" voice is considered to be one of the finest in bluegrass, and between 1949 and 1952, Carter and Ralph recorded songs for Columbia that have become legendary. As Artis writes:

The emotional quality of the Stanley Brothers' voices has never been equaled. It was not forced or theatrical. It was reserved and subtle, but unmistakable and incredibly moving. They were trying to establish themselves as a duet, and their voices blended splendidly in tunes like "It's Never Too Late" and "Too Late to Cry." Probably the most memorable tunes from the Columbia sessions were the trios with Lambert, some of the most hauntingly eerie [high, lonesome singing] ever recorded. Carter wrote most of them and sang them in his distinctively moving way, joined by Ralph on the tenor, with Lambert adding an even higher part: "A Vision of Mother," "Drunkard's Hell," and the classics "White Dove," "The Fields Have Turned Brown," and "The Angels Are Singing." The greatest of these was the chillingly mournful "Lonesome River." [21]

Although Carter died of cancer in 1966, Ralph continued to play throughout the 1990s. The music of the Stanley Brothers is featured in the popular 2000 movie *O Brother, Where Art Thou?*—whose soundtrack has sold millions of CDs.

The Stanley Brothers were among other bluegrass brother acts popular in the 1950s. The Osborne Brothers and Jim & Jesse (McReynolds) also recorded well-loved bluegrass records in the 1950s. Like Carter Stanley, Bobby Osborne did a brief stint with Bill Monroe as a lead vocalist.

Stars of the Folk Revival

When rock and roll was born in the 1950s, the wildly popular new style drew audiences away from bluegrass and country music. But, as Jesse McReynolds states, "the big appeal to bluegrass is that it's live music." [22] By

Parking Lot
Pickers

In Old as the Hills, *Steven D. Price describes amateur and professional musicians at a typical bluegrass festival:*

A festival typically takes place over an entire weekend on grounds encompassing many acres of land suitable for camping. The audience begins to arrive on Friday afternoon, quickly lining the road with their cars, trucks, and campers. No sooner do people reach the ground then they unpack their instruments, raring to locate others with whom to make music. This aspect goes to the very heart of festivals, and indeed of Bluegrass itself. 'Parking lot picker' is the term for an amateur who not only listens to Bluegrass, but who plays it. They're the people who willingly travel hundreds of miles to attend concerts and festivals and who follow the music as closely as stockbrokers scrutinize tickertape. . . .

When the bands' buses pull up, it's as though the circus has come to town. Fans cluster around favorites, expressing their admiration and requesting tunes, while the professionals greet friends and sign autographs. As the dinner hour approaches, the aroma of charcoal lazily spreads across the campgrounds, and then the crowd gathers at a wooden-plank bandstand for the evening concert. . . . Each band does a set of fifteen or twenty minutes. . . . The show ends, and spectators wend their way back to tents, trailers, and sleeping bags. . . .

Professionals have no reluctance about "sitting in" with parking lot pickers, without feeling a need to show off or outshine their colleagues of the moment. Amateurs find the company stimulating and find that they are spurred on to play in ways they never knew they could. This kind of spontaneity and camaraderie marks any festival. Pickers pick and trade licks, listeners listen, vendors sell their wares, and friends gossip, all in a relaxed atmosphere and admixture of lifestyles. Long hair or crew cuts, bare feet or polished shoes, wash-and-wear shirts or tie-dyed tank tops, urban accents or rural drawls—the highest common denominator is a passion for Bluegrass.

the early 1960s outdoor bluegrass festivals began taking the music out of the studios and onto the concert stages of America. At this time young audiences were hungry for "genuine" music, and Flatt & Scruggs, Jim & Jesse, and many others perfectly fit the bill.

The first event booked as a bluegrass festival was held on July 4, 1961, in a park in Luray, Virginia. Until this time bluegrass acts had performed solo or with other country acts, but never together at one show. The Bluegrass Festival, however, booked Bill Monroe, the Stanley Brothers, and Jim & Jesse as well as the Country Gentlemen, Mac Wiseman, and Bill Clifton all on one bill. When the event quickly sold two thousand tickets—a large crowd for the time—a new venue was open for bluegrass music.

In 1965 the tradition continued when Bill Monroe and promoter Ralph Rinzler held the successful First Annual Bluegrass Festival at Fincastle, Virginia. The next year Monroe held his own event in Bean Blossom, Indiana, a place he often played in his early years. The first events were magical, with only three or four thousand people in attendance.

Monroe headlined and often jammed with past members of his band, such as Ralph Stanley and Jesse McReynolds. And the musical entertainment was not limited only to the professionals. From the very beginning, an army of amateur players—called "parking lot pickers"—brought their own instruments to the festival, and impromptu jam sessions took place in parking lots, campgrounds, and picnic areas.

The good times and great music continued to attract people to Bean Blossom, and by the 1980s it had become one of the largest celebrations of bluegrass music anywhere in the world. Today upward of forty thousand people from across the globe descend on the otherwise sleepy town every June ready to listen to the best the bluegrass world has to offer, while picking up their own instruments to join in the fun.

In addition to Bean Blossom, there are bluegrass festivals held in nearly every state in the United States. They are held in rural country locations and in parks under the towering skyscrapers of New York City. The oldest surviving musicians, such as Earl Scruggs, are joined by a new generation, with some pickers as young as four or five years old. And this homegrown American institution may also be found in Japan, England, Scotland, and elsewhere.

Doc Watson

While festivals attracted thousands of customers, some bluegrass musicians such as Arthel "Doc" Watson found their fame on the 1960s folk festival circuit. And what Bill Monroe is to bluegrass mandolin and Earl Scruggs to banjo, Doc Watson is to guitar.

Watson was born in Deep Gap, North Carolina, in 1923 and has been blind since infancy. Like many pickers, he came from a musical family, and by the time he was a teenager, he had taught himself to play. Watson played rockabilly and western swing until he was in his thirties. But because his band did not have a fiddle player, the blind musician learned to pick out the complicated old-time songs on his guitar, playing them "flat pick" style, that is, with a single "plectrum" guitar pick as opposed to finger picks. When Ralph Rinzler heard Watson play, he immediately began booking him at folk festivals and folk clubs, such as Gerde's Folk City in New York's Greenwich Village. By 1963 Watson landed a coveted spot at the Newport Folk Festival sharing the bill with Bill Monroe and others. In later years Watson toured with his son Merle, another hot guitar picker, who died tragically in a tractor accident in 1985.

In the years following Merle's death, Watson began holding a series of benefit concerts in Wilkesboro, North Carolina, to raise money for a memorial garden in honor of his son. The bill was filled by musicians who were colleagues of Merle's. Since the first MerleFest was held in 1988, using two flatbed trucks for stages, it has grown into one of the premier bluegrass and country music festivals in America. By 2002 the festival featured over a hundred legendary country artists and bands, including Alison Krauss, Blue Highway, and Patty Loveless. In addition, folk music from across the globe is represented with musicians from parts of Africa, Ireland, and Louisiana represented in the mix.

By 2002 the musicians were performing to more than forty thousand

Bluegrass guitarist Doc Watson began country music's legendary MerleFest to commemorate his son.

people on nine separate stages. For the parking lot pickers, there were guitar, banjo, and mandolin contests as well as songwriting showcases. In addition to bringing more than $12 million to the local economy, this bluegrass paradise distributes millions of dollars to civic and charity organizations.

Newgrass Music

Merle Watson's contemporaries who play at MerleFest include guitarists Tony Rice and Peter Rowan and mandolin picker Sam Bush. These men were part of a reworking of bluegrass music in the 1970s, and the style took its name from a Bluegrass Alliance album titled *Newgrass.*

Combining bluegrass harmony and rhythm with jazzy licks and counterculture sensibilities, newgrass was brought into the mainstream in 1975 when Grateful Dead guitarist—and part-time banjo picker—Jerry Garcia released the album *Old and in the Way,* with Peter Rowan, mandolin player Dave Grisman, former Blue Grass Boys fiddler Vasser Clements, and bassist John Kahn. As Art Howard writes in the *Atlanta Journal:* "Garcia's recordings were critical in bringing bluegrass to a young, urban

Musicians like Jerry Garcia combined bluegrass with elements of rock and jazz to create "newgrass."

rock audience and paving the way for newgrass. By the late '70's, New Grass Revival, a quartet of longhaired instrumental stars based in Nashville, was stretching the music into the realms of progressive rock and jazz." [23]

In the 1990s the progressive bluegrass tradition was carried on by bands such as Leftover Salmon, who bill their rollicking fusion of bluegrass, rock, and jazz as "polyethnic Cajun slamgrass." [24] The style is also heard in the music of banjo wizard Béla Fleck.

Timeless Quality

From bluegrass to newgrass, the musical style is based on British and Irish fiddle tunes hundreds of years old. Bluegrass was kicked into high gear in the mid–twentieth century by Doc Watson, Bill Monroe, Earl Scruggs, and others. What began as simple string band music in the hills and hollows of Appalachia may be heard today throughout the United States, as well as Japan, Europe, and elsewhere. And while it may be the music of the people, it requires a patient and talented musician to perform the double-quick licks and high, lonesome harmonies true to the style. But there is a sense of joy and wonder—and a timeless quality of an old-time barn dance—wherever the ringing sound of banjos, fiddles, guitars, and mandolins splits the air. Although bluegrass founder Bill Monroe is dead, as Richard D. Smith writes, "this powerful music may go on for centuries. . . . And as long as bluegrass is played, heard, and loved, Mr. Bill Monroe will never have a last day on earth." [25]

Chapter Three

Honky-Tonk Music

While the rapid-fire picking of bluegrass musicians occupies a special place in country, it is the honky-tonk style that lies at the roots of most modern country music. And unlike old-time and bluegrass music, honky-tonk did not originate in the Appalachian Mountains but in the southwestern region of the United States, where thousands of small bars and roadhouses lined the highways catering to rough-and-tumble crowds who earned their paycheck working on "wildcat" oil rigs.

With its working-class roots, honky-tonk has a social as well as a musical history that is important to the style. The term itself was coined in the late 1800s to describe the rowdy taverns that lined the trails of Texas, Oklahoma, and other Southwest locales. On a typical Saturday night, these honky-tonks were filled by hardworking men—and a few women—who had come from miles around to drink, date, dance, and, often, fight.

The first published appearance of the word "honky-tonk" can be traced to an 1894 newspaper in Ardmore, Oklahoma, a town about twenty miles from the Texas border. In the *Daily Ardmorite,* a journalist wrote on the front page that "the honk-a-tonk last night was well attended by ball-heads, bachelors and leading citizens." [26] While it is unclear today who the ball-heads might have been, it is certain that more than a century ago the term was familiar to the rural folks in that corner of Oklahoma.

It was also obvious that songwriters and musicians were quite familiar with honky-tonks. In 1916 two composers wrote a piece of music called "Honky Tonky" that was recorded on Victor Records. In 1918 a New York musical called *Everything* contained the gem "Everything Is Hunky Dory Down in Honky Tonk Town." By the 1920s there was a flood of songs utilizing the term, including "Sister Honky Tonk" and "Honky Tonk Train Blues." By the end

Originating in the 1890s, the term "honky-tonk" was used to describe saloons like the one pictured here.

of the decade, the words had entered the literary world in a Carl Sandburg poem and books by John Steinbeck, William Faulkner, and others.

Oil Field Roughnecks

While Pulitzer Prize–winning authors may have seized upon a poetic term to liven up their stories, the real honky-tonks in the Southwest were anything but pretty. When the Prohibition era ended in 1933, making it legal once again to manufacture and sell alcoholic beverages in the United States, thousands of honky-tonks sprang up in hastily constructed buildings on the long, lonely highways of the Southwest. They were often built a few miles outside of towns, on "the wrong side of the tracks," because people in respectable neighborhoods would not tolerate the roughnecks who flocked to these establishments.

The honky-tonk clientele usually consisted of oil field workers—young, single men who flocked to boomtowns when oil was discovered and moved on when the wells ran dry. After working grueling twelve-hour shifts, they slept in hotels, tents, truck beds, and even under pool tables in honky-tonks. When Saturday night came, this crowd was usually ready for some hard drinking. When far from wives and girlfriends, the drunk and disheartened men in the honky-tonks often ended up fighting with fists, knives, and occasionally guns. Some even called the bars "bloodbuckets."

Some of the honky-tonks had dance floors and live entertainment. Others featured jukeboxes—coin-operated phonographs that allowed listeners to hear their favorite songs for a nickel.

With the harsh realities of their daily lives, honky-tonk patrons did not want to hear old-time country records with their quaint, often upbeat stories and religious messages. After a hard day on the oil rigs, barely scraping by on their small paychecks and missing their loved ones, honky-tonk patrons wanted songs that spoke to their own personal joys and sorrows. And fame and fortune awaited those singers and songwriters who could sing to the honky-tonkers in their own language.

"Girls Jump in Cars"

Al Dexter was quite familiar with the lingo of the honky-tonk, because the songwriter owned the Round-Up Club in Turnertown, Texas. In 1936, when his songwriting partner James B. Paris suggested they pen a tune using the word "honky-tonk," however, Dexter was unfamiliar with the phrase. As Dexter told author Nick Tosches in *Country: The Music and Musicians:*

One day I went to see Paris . . . and he said, "I thought of a title last night that'll set the woods on fire." I asked him what it was, and he said, "Honky Tonk Blues." I asked him where he got that idea. I never heard the word, so I said, "What is a honky-tonk?" So he said, "These beer joints up and

down the road where the girls jump in cars and so on." I said, "Never thought about it like that." He said, "Use your thinker-upper [brain] and let's write a song like that." [27]

Apparently Paris had put a good idea in his "thinker-upper" because the team's "Honky Tonk Blues" helped define the style that would remain popular well into the twenty-first century. While Dexter sings about the blues he can't lose because of his honky-tonk girl, two electric guitars create a rhythm like a Model A Ford bouncing rapidly down the highway. The lead guitar break combines hot single-note picking over jazz chords that give the feel of the warm Texas breeze. And, unlike the acoustic instruments of old-time music, the recorded sounds of the electric bass and amplified guitars were perfect for cutting through the noisy din of the boisterous honky-tonks.

"Honky Tonk Blues" was a hit, and within a few years, even staunch traditionalists like Roy Acuff were performing numbers such as "Honky Tonk Mamas."

In 1941 the first million-selling honky-tonk hit was Ernest Tubb's "Walking the Floor Over You." Tubb, born in 1914 in Crisp, Texas—about forty miles from Dallas—centered his early career on imitating Jimmie Rodgers, whose depression-era songs about Texas, railroad trains, and the homesick blues inspired a generation of honky-tonkers.

Texas Honky-Tonks in the 1930s

In his book Texas My Texas, *excerpted on the "Virtual Texan" website, James Ward Lee describes the evolution of honky-tonks in the 1930s:*

When the [Prohibition Act] was repealed in 1933, America was already criss-crossed by a network of all-weather roads and populated by a million Fords, Chevrolets, Studebakers, Willyses, and Plymouths. There was nothing for it but to begin a crash program of roadhouse construction. A few miles outside hundreds of Texas towns, slab-sided buildings were suddenly thrown up. . . . Some of the more affluent owners built a few outhouse-sized "tourist" cabins in the event that men and women "of questionable repute" . . . should decide to seek shelter from the night air.

[Even] in the areas where there was no oil . . . [coal] miners, mill hands, plantworkers, and even small merchants and clerks flocked to the roadhouses being built on the outskirts of small towns and big cities alike. The working orders went to drink the recently legalized beer—ten cents for local beer, fifteen cents for national brands—to dance to the hillbilly music played by ol' boys who worked by day and picked by night, and to mingle with their own kind. . . .

By the end of the thirties, the jukebox had almost completely replaced live music except on weekends. The magnificent Rock-ola "music-machine," could hold as many as twelve records, twenty-four songs. And it only cost a nickel to play . . . any of the . . . hits of the late Depression. As the records spun out their two-and-a-half minutes of magic, the machines were kaleidoscopes of colored lights, shifting liquid, and moving air bubbles. By the eve of World War II, the music played in honky tonks had changed. . . . The new amplified music of Ernest Tubb made it possible for even the deafest to hear the songs, and who would dare miss every word of "Walking the Floor Over You"?

Although Tubb was only nineteen years old when Rodgers died in 1933, the Texas singer befriended the "Singing Brakeman's" widow, Carrie. She liked Tubb's style and loaned the lanky singer Rodgers's suit coat for early photographs and, more important, his sweet-sounding Martin guitar for recording sessions. Tubb's early imitations of Rodgers did not sell. But, as Tosches writes:

> Something had happened: Ernest Tubb had begun to discover his own voice. Instead of trying to duplicate the vocal mannerisms and style of his idol, he had begun to express, in his natural way, the sensibilities he had absorbed from Rodgers. At the same time, Tubb had become aware of the new barroom music called honky-tonk. By this time . . . Tubb had opened a honky-tonk of his own, the E&E Tavern. The honky-tonk music he heard was lively but insubstantial. If Rodgers had taught him anything, it was that music without power—be it the power of meanness, the power of love, the power of sentimentality, the power of sadness or madness, sweetness or venom—was music without worth. Ernest Tubb was on his way to empowering country music and recasting honky-tonk with his own new-found voice, a voice that was the sum of all he had learned from the master, and from himself. And he was on his way to glory. [28]

When "Walking the Floor Over You" was released in the summer of 1941, it went to number one, selling more than 400,000 copies in a few months. And it was the first country "crossover" hit, that is, it sold to both country and mainstream popular, or "pop," audiences. Tubb, who had been struggling in the music business for years, became an "overnight sensation," taking honky-tonk music to the stage of the *Grand Ole Opry* and appearing in a few Hollywood movies. He continued to score hits such as "Drivin' Nails in My Coffin" and "Let's Say Goodbye Like We Said Hello" that remain honky-tonk classics today.

Ernest Tubb brought the lively honky-tonk sound to mainstream audiences.

Honky-Tonk Everywhere

America entered World War II in December 1941, and the Texas honky-tonks began to empty as millions of men joined the military. The music remained vibrant, however, as honky-tonk stars such as Tubb and others played USO tours for military personnel. These shows in the United States and overseas exposed country performers to northern audiences who had previously ignored or scorned what they referred to as "hillbilly" music. And country music was bigger than ever. In fact, marines fighting in Asia reported that Japanese soldiers would taunt them by insulting the president, a national baseball hero, and "the King of Country Music," screaming "To hell with Roosevelt! To hell with Babe Ruth! To hell with Roy Acuff!"[29]

On the home front honky-tonk continued to sell. In 1942 Dexter scored his first crossover hit with "Pistol Packin' Mama," which sold even more records than "Walking the Floor Over You." The phenomenon of "Pistol Packin' Mama" is described by Kurt Wolff in *Country Music: The Rough Guide:*

> "Pistol Packin' Mama" made Al Dexter . . . a household name in the 1940s. A bouncy little number about a gal who barges into a tavern looking to gun down her cheating man, it sold a million well before the year was out. . . . It boiled out of nearly every jukebox in the nation . . . and was covered by some of the biggest pop singers of the day, including Bing Crosby and Frank Sinatra.

His "Mama" wasn't kidding around when she "filled him full of lead," but Dexter sure sounded like he was having a jolly good time recording "Pistol Packin' Mama." Despite the bitterness and violence that burns through the song's lyrics ("she kicked out my windshield and hit me over the head"), Dexter delivered them with a smile on his face.[30]

With his hit topping the charts, Dexter often toured in California, where tens of thousands of southerners had recently moved to work in the defense industry. And the southern migration to California was staggering—in the San Francisco Bay area alone, 29 percent of newcomers came from Arkansas, Louisiana, Texas, and Oklahoma. Similar numbers of recent immigrants existed in the Los Angeles and San Diego areas. To cater to the demand, roadside honky-tonks opened near defense plants and military bases. Meanwhile, radio programmers saw gold in honky-tonk, and nearly every major California station featured barn dance shows and country music acts.

With country "going Hollywood," it was inevitable that performers' clothing would become more glamorous. A Russian tailor named Nutya "Nudie" Cohn aided this process when he opened a shop in his Los Angeles garage and became one of the first people to sew fake diamonds, called rhinestones, onto western suits. By the end of the decade, Nudie had moved to Hollywood and nearly every honky-tonk singer who

Rhinestone Cowboys

In Country Music: The Rough Guide, *Kurt Wolff relates the history of rhinestone-covered Nudie suits popular with honky-tonk performers since the late 1940s.*

While top business executives prefer subdued gray flannel suits, country music stars have often reached into their closets for something a bit louder—like an electric turquoise suit with matching stetson [hat] and boots, studded with rhinestones and embroidered with big gold coins and dollar bills. These flamboyantly decorated outfits in peacock colors are generically called "Nudie suits," after Ukrainian-born, Brooklyn-bred tailor . . . Nudie Cohn . . . the western-wear specialist best known for creating them.

Serving as both performance costumes and status symbols, Nudie-style suits are typically embroidered, studded, sequined and spangled with motifs big enough to be seen in the back row of any auditorium. The simplest are trimmed with names, initials, or a pattern of musical notes and guitars. Western images such as cactuses, six-shooters, prairie flowers, or arrows and teepees are also popular. Some outfits play off a performer's name: Porter Wagoner's suits are decked out with wagon wheels, Ferlin Husky's with husky dogs. Other costumes plug hit songs. Nudie made . . . a suit covered with locks, keys and prison bars for Webb Pierce when "In the Jailhouse Now" topped the charts. . . .

In 1947, Nudie was able to open his own shop in Hollywood. By that stage, the fashions worn by silver-screen cowboys had been adopted by many hillbilly performers who'd never been west of the Mississippi. These country stars loved Nudie's show-biz flair (he'd once sewn G-strings and costumes for strippers in New York), and each custom suit from his shop seemed more outrageous than the last. . . . Among his best-known creations are the $10,000 24-karat gold lamé tuxedo worn by Elvis Presley.

had achieved success had a shimmering Nudie suit in his or her wardrobe.

Travis Picking

One of the hottest West Coast guitar slingers was Kentucky-born Merle Travis, who preferred double-breasted suits over Nudie's rhinestones. His guitar playing, however, was as flashy as Nudie's wildest suit.

Travis was born in the heart of Kentucky coal country, and his songs, such

The Bakersfield Sound

California remained influential in country music throughout the 1950s and '60s. As the hard-edged honky-tonk sound began to soften in the '60s, a group of artists in Bakersfield, California, pioneered the "Bakersfield Sound," which had a raw twang of the "chicken-picking" guitar and a rocking honky-tonk sound backed by the pedal steel.

The king of the Bakersfield Sound was Buck Owens, who was actually born in Texas but moved with his family to Bakersfield in the early '50s. With his band, the Buckaroos, Owens made his first honky-tonk recordings for Capitol Records in Los Angeles in 1956, adding up-tempo rock rhythms for a new fast-paced blend of country. Singing and playing his trademark electric guitar, a Fender Telecaster, and backed by lead player Don Rich on his Telecaster, Owens had a string of hits beginning with the 1963 "Act Naturally," later covered by the Beatles and hundreds of other performers. After that breakthrough, Owens had fourteen consecutive number one records on the country charts until 1967 and a total of twenty chart toppers until 1972. Although he was world famous, Owens refused to abandon Bakersfield, which was soon nicknamed "Buckersfield."

Merle Haggard was a true Bakersfield native who—in addition to serving two years in prison for burglary—was well known for his singing abilities in his hometown honky-tonks. In 1967 Haggard penned his first major hit, "Swingin' Doors," and continued to top country charts with songs such as the anti-counterculture song "Okie from Muskogee" and the semi-autobiographical "Mama Tried," about turning twenty-one in prison. Today the Bakersfield legend continues at Buck Owens's Crystal Palace, a $7 million museum, concert hall, and restaurant. From its humble origins in 1950s Bakersfield, the sounds of Haggard, Owens, and others have traveled across the globe.

as "Sixteen Tons" and "Dark as a Dungeon," are odes to the suffering faced by coal miners. Travis also wrote humorous songs such as "Smoke! Smoke! Smoke! (That Cigarette)," "Divorce Me C.O.D.," and "So Round, So Firm, So Fully Packed." While that alone would have landed him in the Country Music Hall of Fame, Travis was also known for his unique thumb-picking guitar style, now known as "Travis picking," in which the thumb plays a steady rhythm of bass notes while the first and second fingers play the melody on the higher strings. While Travis may not have invented the style, he played it with a skill few can match.

Beauty, Truth, and Pain

While the honky-tonkers were pioneering their own sound in California, singer-songwriter Hank Williams was making a name for himself appearing on barn dance radio shows and touring "bloodbucket" honky-tonk bars in his native Alabama.

Williams was born in rural Butler County, Alabama, in 1923. After a poverty-stricken childhood, Williams learned to play music from an African American street musician named Rufus "Tee-Tot" Payne in the tiny town of Georgiana. By the time he was eighteen, Williams was performing on local radio stations and had put together a band playing Roy Acuff covers and original tunes.

Williams loved to drink, however, and by the time he was nineteen, his life closely paralleled the suffering and torment he would later make famous in the words to his songs. Williams deeply loved his young wife, Audrey Mae Sheppard, but their union was marked by chaos, as Wolff writes:

> Hank first met . . . Sheppard while he was touring with a medicine show in southern Alabama. A year later they were married, and almost just as quickly the arguing

began, usually fueled by Hank's appetite for booze. Drinking was a habit that would land Hank in jail, dry-docked in a sanatorium, and face down in the gutter many times over.[31]

In 1949 Williams went to Nashville to record the 1920s yodeled lament "Lovesick Blues," a song that perfectly encapsulated the pain of his relationship with his beautiful wife. The song about crying the blues was Williams's first big hit and stayed on the country charts for forty-two weeks. It also earned the singer a spot on the *Grand Ole Opry,* where he was warmly received.

Using his stormy life for songwriting material, Williams penned a string of

Hank Williams's tragic life and early death made him one of country music's most legendary artists.

classics such as "Cold Cold Heart," "You Win Again," "Why Don't You Love Me," "I'm So Lonesome I Could Cry," and "Your Cheatin' Heart." These songs were hits on the country charts, and many were recorded by pop artists. But fame and fortune meant little to Williams, who sank into a deep depression while his wife went out with other men. As Tosches writes:

> [By 1952] Hank was in the worst shape of his life, living in physical and emotional wretchedness at his mother's boardinghouse in Montgomery [Alabama]. He pined for his faithless wife, Miss Audrey, drank, took [the dangerous tranquilizer] chloral hydrate, drank, fell down and cracked his skull, [drank] some more, and wrote "I'll Never Get Out of This World Alive." [32]

In October 1952, while remaining married to "Miss Audrey," Williams married another woman—onstage at the New Orleans Municipal Auditorium, in front of fourteen thousand paying customers. This stunt did little to make him happy, however. On January 1, 1953, Williams died in the back of a limousine on the way to a concert in Canton, Ohio. His death was attributed to an overdose of tranquilizers and alcohol. He was twenty-nine.

Williams's miserable existence paved the way for a songwriting legacy that influenced every honky-tonk singer who followed, as Wolff writes:

If any single artist captures the essence of country music—has the ability to conjure its emotional turmoil and rustic, earthy beauty in a handful of notes and a few turns of phrase—it must surely be Hank Williams. Country music was already in the midst of a honky-tonk revolution . . . but when this wiry young Alabama singer arrived on the stage of the *Grand Ole Opry* in 1949, the music burst its seams, foamed at the mouth, and was never the same beast again.

Though Hank was on the surface a raw and untrained singer, he was also an incredibly expressive one, his voice yipping, breaking, moaning and almost choking on each word, big or small. Locked into each crack and dip of his southern twang was a beauty and truth, pure and very real. . . .

His songs hit raw nerves with spine-chilling effect, yet at the same time they were so beautiful a person could sit down and weep from the sheer joy of their simple but awesome power. Never had pain and sadness sounded so damn good. [33]

Stars who die tragically at the height of their careers often become legends, and Williams was no exception. His personal, introspective songs permanently changed the sound of country and paved the way for a new generation of honky-tonk singers such as Lefty Frizzell, Webb Pierce, Ray Price, Faron Young, Hank Snow, and George Jones.

Honky-Tonk Angels

The drinking, cheating, lovesick blues were not confined to men after Tennessee native Kitty Wells burst onto the scene. Wells started her musical career singing backup vocals for her husband, struggling country artist Johnnie Wright. Although she was about to retire from the music business to be a full-time mother at the age of thirty-three, a record producer persuaded her

Known as the "Queen of Country Music," Kitty Wells led the way for many female country music artists.

to record "It Wasn't God Who Made Honky Tonk Angels." The song was written in response to the line from honky-tonk star Hank Thompson's song "The Wild Side of Life," in which he sings, "I didn't know God made honky tonk angels/I might have known you'd never make a wife," to which Wells responded: "It wasn't God who made honky-tonk angels /As you said in the words of your song/ Too many times married men think they're still single / That has caused many a good girl to go wrong."[34]

"Honky Tonk Angels" shot to number one and stayed there for six weeks in 1952. Wells went on to record more than a dozen hits in the 1950s and early '60s, earning her the title "Queen of Country Music." Meanwhile, honky-tonk music suddenly had a female voice. As country superstar Loretta Lynn said:

> First time I heard [Kitty Wells] I thought there was an angel singing. . . . I thought, "Gee, here the women are starting to sing!" It was such a treat to hear a woman sing. I think with that song she touched in me what I was living and what I was going through and I knew there was a lot of women that lived like me. I thought, "Here's a woman telling our point of view of everyday life." You know, women staying home at night while the guy's going out for a card game. Game didn't last all night, but the men did. Men going

out with the boys, but they're not out with the boys. It was something nobody else was writing or singing about. It really got to me. I thought, "This is a great thing." So I started writing songs. [35]

As soon as "Honky Tonk Angels" became a hit, Nashville producers were eager to find other female vocalists who could match the success of Wells. They found one in Patsy Cline, a hard-drinking rowdy hell-raiser who was a true honky-tonk angel, having learned about the world while singing in dingy bars from the time she was sixteen.

Cline's first success came after she sang "Walkin' After Midnight" on the popular *Arthur Godfrey's Talent Scouts*

Country music artist Patsy Cline in the early years of her career.

on television. In 1960 "I Fall to Pieces" went to number one on the country charts and crossed over to the pop charts, rising to number twelve. And Cline's singing could grab the attention of any listener, as Tosches writes: "Her voice was a big, astounding thing, capable of yodeling merrily, growling the blues, sobbing with emotion, and vaulting octaves with ease. She could transform even second-rate material into emotional essays." [36]

Like Hank Williams, Cline died tragically at the height of her career, although not because of self-destructive behavior. On March 5, 1963, while returning home from a concert, her private plane crashed in bad weather in Tennessee. Cline continues to live on in her music, however, influencing countless female country, pop, and rock vocalists throughout the years.

Cline, Williams, and Wells are the best known honky-tonk heroes from the music's heyday. But they were joined by dozens of others, such as Floyd Tillman, Red Foley, Hankshaw Hawkins, Red Sovine, and others too numerous to name. While the music was based on simple three-chord progressions, it took the emotional, and sometimes tragic, lives of the singers to give the songs true meaning. Today the honky-tonk style remains popular because of stars such as John Anderson, Dwight Yoakam, George Strait, Clint Black, and others. And as long as there are broken hearts, lonesome highways, and honky-tonk bars, the music will remain as vital as it was in the long-lost Texas of the 1930s.

Chapter Four

Cowboy Music and Western Swing

The songs of Hank Williams, Patsy Cline, and others helped make honky-tonk the most popular music of the 1940s and early '50s. With simple melodies and basic instrumentation, honky-tonk was music that was easy to understand.

Another type of country, western swing, paralleled the rise of honky-tonk. This big band music, with complex, layered arrangements, was greatly influenced by two seemingly opposing cultures—cowboys and African American jazz players. And acting as a catch-all for musical styles, western swing also embodied the sounds of hoedown fiddles, folk music, blues, Tin Pan Alley pop, Mexican folk, and Louisiana Cajun music. From this amalgam, "cowboy jazz" topped the country charts for nearly thirty years.

While embracing so many styles, western swing is literally big band music, with more than a dozen players in popular groups such as Bob Wills and

His Texas Playboys. The lineup might include several singers accompanied by a piano, mandolin, bass, and drum, along with several fiddles, guitars, trumpets, and saxophones.

While band members dressed in western shirts, cowboy boots, and Stetson hats, they were actually playing chords and lead breaks that owed more to urban jazz than hillbilly records. The western flavor was added by the fiddles and pedal steel guitars, along with lyrics about San Antonio, Amarillo, and Tulsa. And in the years before rock and roll, western swing rocked the dance hall with an irresistible beat.

Genuine Singing Cowboys

The roots of western swing lie in the cultural mix of early twentieth-century Texas, where white southerners intermingled with African Americans, Mexicans, and recent German immigrants. But Texas was, above all, cowboy country, and the men who earned their pay rounding up, roping, and branding

Bob Wills and his Texas Playboys play to an audience in Oceanpark, California.

cattle were romanticized throughout the United States in dime novels, silent films, and folk songs.

In the 1920s, with the commercialization of hillbilly music in the record and radio industries, a few Texans were able to bring their traditional cowboy songs to a wider audience. One of the first men to earn the title of "Singing Cowboy" on the radio was Jules Verne Allen, who grew up working on a cattle ranch in Waxahachie, Texas, and later became a broncobuster in Montana. Throughout the 1920s and '30s, Allen, who billed himself as "Longhorn Luke" performed on radio stations throughout the West, singing songs that reflected the roughrider life he had experienced. He recorded songs such as "The Cowtrail to Mexico,"

"Little Joe, the Wrangler," and "The Cowboy's Dream," that helped popularize cowboy music across the United States.

Another cowboy who sang from experience was Goebel Reeves, the "Texas Drifter." Although his father was in the Texas legislature, Reeves left his pampered life to travel around the United States as a hobo. This hard-traveling tradition was shared by other country singers at the time, such as Cliff Carlisle and Harry McClintock. As Bill C. Malone writes in *Country Music, U.S.A.*: "When these men sang of dank prison cells, brutal cops, rattling freight trains, and lonely and hungry hours, they spoke with authority and assurance. Nowhere does the authentic voice of the folk experience stand out more clearly than in the recordings of these singers." [37] Reeves recorded his experiences in now-classic songs such as "Hobo's Lullaby" and "The Cowboy's Prayer." McClintock gained notice with cowboy classics such as "Jesse James," "Texas Rangers," and "Goodbye Old Paint," a farewell to a favorite horse. McClintock's recording of "Big Rock Candy Mountain" made him famous in the 1920s. And although the singer

"Haywire" McClintock

Harry "Haywire" McClintock was a roving songwriter who led an extremely interesting life, as Kurt Wolff writes in Country Music: The Rough Guide:

McClintock wasn't your average cowboy singer. He wasn't your average anything, in fact. Born in Knoxville, Tennessee in 1882, he left home as a teenager to ride the rails and see the world. . . . In addition to making music, he held an assortment of odd jobs during his lifetime, including cowboy, mule driver, seaman and journalist. "Haywire Mac," a nickname he picked up along the way, recorded more than forty sides for Victor, but he became well known as a pioneering radio personality. . . .

Mac picked up all sorts of classic old-time cowboy songs while working as a cow puncher, and he recorded quite a few, such as "The Old Chisholm Trail" and "Sam Bass." But he was also an active member of the [union advocacy group] Industrial Workers of the World and wrote and sang many songs with labor and social themes. McClintock is best remembered, however, for a pair of hobo songs, "Hallelujah! I'm a Bum" and "Big Rock Candy Mountain." Both became hobo camp mainstays and survived in folk circles for decades afterwards. . . .

Mac's hobo songs (another was titled "The Bum Song") were gritty and unflinching on the one hand, yet also presented a good-natured view of the wanderer's lifestyle—which was a common experience at the time, as many young men rode the rails both as a way to see the world and as a means to travel between jobs. "Hallelujah" isn't so much a ballad on the perils of homelessness as it is a celebration of the hobo lifestyle—something the protagonist has adopted by choice. "I don't like work, and work don't like me," sings McClintock, "and that is the reason I'm so hungry."

died in 1957, the song was featured in the 2000 *O Brother, Where Art Thou?*—a film whose soundtrack was nominated for a Country Music Association (CMA) "Album of the Year" award in 2001.

Hollywood Cowboys

As soon as they began making films with sound in 1928, Hollywood film directors were quick to pick up on the singing cowboy trend. The first genuine horse-riding songster to appear on the silver screen was trick rider Ken Maynard, who sang traditional trailside songs such as "The Lone Star Trail"

Gene Autry became popular in Hollywood films with his portrayal of a singing cowboy.

and "The Cowboy's Lament" in the 1929 film *The Wagon Master.*

Gene Autry, the superstar of the singing cowboys, was actually a telegraph operator for the railroad in Sapupla, Oklahoma. Autry's claim to fame was that he could closely imitate Jimmie Rodgers's yodeling style. After he lost his office job when the depression hit in 1929, Autry rode the rails to New York City where he walked up and down the streets with his guitar, begging record executives for auditions. He finally recorded an album for Victor titled *Oklahoma's Singing Cowboy,* which landed him a spot on the influential WLS *National Barn Dance* radio show in Chicago, where he was immensely popular. By 1934 Autry was in Hollywood making movies as the "Nation's Number One Singing Cowboy."[38] He eventually made more than a hundred films and became the most famous singing cowboy in the world. As Malone writes:

> Not only did he become quite wealthy, but he created the stereotype of the heroic cowboy who was equally adept with a gun and guitar. Autry was not the first individual to sing in a western movie . . . but he was the first to attract any national attention. With Autry ensconced as a singing movie cowboy, hillbilly music now had a new medium through which to popularize itself. The Silver Screen romanticized the cowboy and helped to develop the idea of western music.[39]

Bob Wills appears here with Tommy Duncan, the guitarist/vocalist of his group the Texas Playboys.

The influence of the singing cowboys on western music was immense. Hollywood producers began searching for other cowboy acts to rival Autry, and dozens of country bands, hoping to become famous, dropped their traditional hillbilly repertoire, bought cowboy outfits, and adopted names such as the Riders of the Purple Sage, the Girls of the Golden West, and the Cowboy Ramblers. Three men formed the Sons of the Pioneers and wrote classics such as "Cool Water" and "Tumbling Tumble Weeds," although they were from Canada, Ohio, and Missouri. Even Tin Pan Alley writers in New York who had never been west of New Jersey began to turn out cowboy hits such as "I'm an Old Cowhand" and "Home in Wyoming."

The Father of Western Swing

One of the more popular cowboy groups to appear in films was Bob Wills and His Texas Playboys. But Wills got his start long before Gene Autry and others won the West on the silver screen.

Wills played his first gig in 1915, at the age of ten, when his fiddling father, John, got drunk and failed to appear at a ranch dance near his home in Turkey, Texas. Young Bob showed up instead and sawed out the only six songs he knew by heart. The cowpokes, ranch hands, and assembled ladies first laughed at the small boy but were soon dancing.

Wills continued to play his music, combining the old-time fiddle breakdowns that his relatives had brought to Texas from Appalachia with African American blues and Dixieland jazz. Wills learned these styles from local black musicians with whom he worked side by side in the cotton fields from the time he was three years old. In fact, he loved black performers so much he rode his pony fifty miles to see a concert by singer Bessie Smith, "the Empress of the Blues."

By the time he was twenty-five, Wills was pioneering "western jazz"—intermingling his old-time fiddle licks with sliding notes, syncopation, improvisation, and the heavy Dixieland beat found in jazz and blues music.

In 1930 the fiddling Wills began playing regularly on radio shows in Fort Worth. He added singer Milton Brown to the Wills Fiddle Band, which included two guitarists and a piano and banjo player. Influenced by the wildly popular jazz music of the time, the Wills Fiddle Band was a pumped-up string band that utilized dance hall rhythms while trading lightning-fast riffs. When the band landed a sought-after gig on a radio program sponsored by Light Crust Flour, they became the Light Crust Doughboys.

Although the Doughboys were popular, their small success was hampered by Wills, who would occasionally disappear on weeklong drinking binges, causing the band to miss radio shows and dance engagements. Although these outbreaks with alcoholism were rare—Wills remained sober most of the time—key band members quit after the Doughboys were fired from the radio show.

In 1933 Wills put together a band he named Bob Wills and His Texas Playboys. It consisted of Wills on fiddle, joined by a vocalist, pianist, bassist, rhythm guitarist, and steel guitar player.

"What Makes Bob Holler?"

Between 1934 and 1942, the Texas Playboys worked out of Tulsa, Oklahoma, and played a continual series of radio and dance shows. In a 1935 recording session in Dallas, Wills utilized a thirteen-piece band that included trumpet, saxophone, clarinet, trombone, and a trio of violinists. The fiddle players learned jazz licks from the horn players, and this incarnation of the Texas Playboys was the first to play true to the style that would later be labeled western swing.

In retrospect, this experiment seemed musically logical, but at the time it generated quite a bit of controversy. For example, the Tulsa musicians' union refused to let the Texas Playboys join because they ruled that

King of the Steel Guitar

The signature sound of western swing is the steel guitar, an instrument developed in Hawaii during the nineteenth century when indigenous musicians became fascinated with the wave-like sound of the picked notes and the slide bar moving up and down the strings. The steel guitar, played horizontally while resting on the musician's lap, moved east, and by the 1930s it was a fixture in western swing bands.

One of the most famous steel guitar players was Leon McAuliffe, who played with Bob Wills and His Texas Playboys. His biography is printed on the website "Leon McAuliffe— Western Swing's Most Famous Steel Guitarist":

During the heyday of Western Swing music the phrase "Take it away Leon," nearly became a household phrase in the south. It was spoken by Bob Wills and referred to Leon McAuliffe, one of the best and most famous steel guitarists in the world. . . .

William Leon McAuliffe was born in Houston, Texas, on March 1, 1917. He began playing both Hawaiian and standard guitar at age 14. He began appearing on a local radio station as part of the group the Waikiki Strummers in 1931. Two years later he joined [the] Light Crust Doughboys. . . . He learned to electronically amplify his guitar from Houston's Bob Dunn, a member of Milton Brown's Musical Brownies. Fiddler Jesse Ashlock invited the 18-year-old McAuliffe to join Bob Wills' Texas Playboys in 1935. He remained with the band for many years, recording many songs, moving to California, and even appearing in several motion pictures.

His signature song was "Steel Guitar Rag," a tune he apparently adapted from a combination of Sylvester Weaver's "Guitar Rag" and part of the Hawaiian song "On the Beach at Waikiki.". . . McAuliffe was one of the first people to use multineck steel guitars, with each neck tuned differently.

Western swing guitarist Leon McAuliffe at his home in Rodgers, Arkansas.

what Wills played was not music and, by extension, the Playboys were not musicians. Despite this prejudice, the Playboys were some of the hottest—and most entertaining—musicians around.

The music of the Texas Playboys was, above all, dance music. It revolved around the fiddles, but Wills tried to distance himself from the "hillbilly" label and instead sought to project an air of musical sophistication and class. The band played blues songs such as "Sittin' on Top of the World," Jimmie Rodgers's compositions such as "Blue Yodel No. 1," and jazzy numbers such as "Osage Stomp." Despite this eclectic repertoire, the music was fun, as Kurt Wolff writes:

> For all its sophistication, the Playboys' music was also wild, loose and free of stylistic constraints. When twin fiddles, guitars, horns and drums fired into song, "rowdy" was definitely part of the agenda. The players were superb, and one by one each would take solos that boggled the minds of the spectators and dancers. Western swing was all about fun and good times, and Wills' whoops, "ahh-haa"'s [sic], and interjections of "play that trombone, boy" or "take it away, Leon" when each man stepped to the mike gave the whole experience a playful feeling. . . . To the public all this tomfoolery and brazen showing-off gave the proceedings familiarity.

Cindy Walker even wrote a song for the Playboys titled "What Makes Bob Holler?" that poked gentle fun at Wills' uninhibited commentary; it became a Playboys standard.[40]

The band played an eclectic mix of country standards, fiddle tunes, blues, and jazz, and their records had something to please everyone. By 1940 the Texas Playboys were competing with popular horn-based swing bands led by Tommy Dorsey, Glenn Miller, and Benny Goodman. And the band continued to grow—in 1943 there were twenty-two members of the Texas Playboys including four fiddles and a full brass section that included five saxophones, two clarinets, and two trumpets. The sound may have been urban jazz, but the lyrics about Blue Bonnet Lane, the rose of San Antonio, and faded love were strictly country.

By this time Wills's popularity had moved beyond the Southwest, and his songs such as "New San Antonio Rose" were stocked on more than 300,000 jukeboxes nationwide. His live concerts were attended by upward of fifteen hundred people—a large number at the time—and Wills was the highest-paid leader of any band in the country. Like many other so-called singing cowboys, Wills soon made it out to Hollywood, where his entire band appeared in the 1941 film *Go West, Young Lady*. The next year Wills was hired by Columbia Pictures to appear in eight films. Flush with success, the fiddler from Turkey,

Bob Wills's *For the Last Time*

By 1970 Bob Wills had been fiddling for appreciative audiences for fifty-five years. On May 30 of that year, he was honored by the Texas House and Senate for his musical contributions. The next day he had a stroke that paralyzed his right side and made it difficult for him to speak. He improved steadily for the next several years, and at one gig in his honor, played the fiddle with his left hand while another player worked the bow.

In December 1973 Wills decided he wanted to assemble the old Texas Playboys for one more recording session. The result was a double LP titled *For the Last Time* (later re-released as a single CD).

Although they hadn't played together in thirty years, the Playboys expertly ran through Wills's classics such as "Texas Playboy Theme," "What Makes Bob Holler?" "San Antonio Rose," "Bubbles in My Beer," and "Big Balls in Cowtown." They were joined on the vocals by country superstar Merle Haggard, a huge Wills fan since childhood. Meanwhile, Wills sat in the middle of the room in his wheelchair beaming with joy and throwing in an occasional "Ahhhhh-ha!"

After six songs Wills began to tire, and Betty, his wife of thirty-two years, took him home. That night Wills had another stroke and lost his ability to move or speak. While he lay in the hospital, the Playboys continued recording—now with new determination to bring the old songs alive again. Wills was unconscious when *For the Last Time* was released in 1974 but clung to life until May 1975. Music was a way of life for Wills, who refused to compromise regardless of commercial pressure. Today *For the Last Time* stands as an unshakable testimony to the man who pioneered western swing.

Texas, moved to California and assembled his dream band stocked with twenty-four of the hottest players in the country.

Wills continued to fill auditoriums and concert halls throughout the 1950s and '60s until poor health caused him to retire around the time he was inducted into the Country Music Hall of Fame in 1968.

The Musical Brownies

Bob Wills may have been one of the founding fathers of western swing—and one of the most commercially successful—but he certainly was not alone. And it is even possible that Wills's fame would have been less if one of his main competitors, singer Milton Brown, had not died in an automobile accident in 1936, well before reaching his prime. It was Brown—backed by Wills on fiddle—who recorded the first true western swing songs "Nancy Jane" and "Sunbonnet Sue," under the band name Fort Worth Doughboys. Like Wills, Brown loved to "holler" during his songs, and on "Nancy Jane," he can be heard exclaiming, "'Oh Nancy!' (twice) and 'Ah ha, she's killing me!'"[41]

Brown was a founding member of the Light Crust Doughboys with Wills, until he took off on his own in 1932. After those first recordings, he formed Milton Brown and His Musical Brownies, a band that rivaled Wills in Texas. The popularity of the band was boosted by the addition of Bob Dunn, whose electric steel guitar was the first amplified instrument used in country music. Fellow musician Jimmy Thomason recalls how Dunn learned to amplify his guitar while jamming at Coney Island in New York: "[He] ran into this black guy who was playing a steel guitar with a homemade pickup attached to it. He had this thing hooked up through an old radio or something and was playing these blues licks. Well, this just knocked Bob out and he got this guy to show him how he was doing it."[42]

When Dunn took the guitar back to Texas, he was the only musician in the state to possess such an instrument. Even without the pedal steel, however, the Brownies produced a unique and original blend of music. Record producers did not fail to notice, and the band recorded over a hundred songs in four years—producing fifty songs in one marathon recording session in March 1936.

Meanwhile, the Brownies were "blowing the roof off" nightclubs and packing in huge crowds, as Wolff writes:

The Brownies' hot, swinging dance music struck a chord with people all over the state who were suffering through the Depression. The music was hot and loose, with a mixture of fiddle, piano and guitar playing, a Dixieland-style rhythm, Dunn's amplified steel and Brown's smooth lead vocals. They played familiar jazz tunes like "St. Louis Blues," sentimental ditties ("My Mary"), novelty songs ("Somebody's Been Using That Thing"), and steaming-hot Mexican-flavored numbers like "In El Rancho Grande." At his peak Brown's songs were wild, juicy and almost out of control—the instrumentalist firmly tethered to the rhythm, yet at the same time appearing to barely hang on.[43]

The Brownies brand of hot western swing came to a sudden end with the car accident that killed Milton Brown. While he was alive, the Brownies never gained much fame beyond the Southwest. It would take Bob Wills and His

Texas Playboys to carry the sound out to the world that the fiddler and the singer had pioneered together selling Light Crust Flour on the radio show.

Melting Pot Music

While Milton Brown and Bob Wills pioneered the sounds of western swing, they were joined by others, including two of Bob's brothers, Billy Jack Wills and Johnnie Lee Wills, both of whom performed and recorded in the shadow of their famous brother.

On the West Coast, fiddler Spade Cooley made a name for himself, leading a large swing band in Southern California. Cooley's band perfected a smoother, more polished sound using written musical arrangements as opposed to improvised jazz licks.

Other names from western swing's golden years were Tex Williams, former vocalist with Cooley, and Pee Wee King and His Golden West Cowboys, who scored a huge hit with "Tennessee Waltz," although Pee Wee King was actually an accordion player raised on polka music in Milwaukee, Wisconsin.

World War II had a negative effect on western swing bands and big band music in general. Many musicians were drafted or joined the military, and bandleaders had to get by with a smaller number of musicians, many of whom lacked the skill of their predecessors. And after the war, the age of swing was over, as millions of musicians married and settled down to raise families, making it difficult to put together touring bands.

Western swing might have passed into oblivion if not for a 1970s revival of the style by "longhair" cowboys in bands such as Commander Cody and His Lost Planet Airmen and Asleep at the Wheel. Cody's large band of virtuoso musicians played many styles including western swing, honky-tonk, blues, Cajun, and rockabilly songs such

Johnnie Lee Wills, brother of Bob Wills, made his own contribution to western swing with his inspired violin playing.

as "Hot Rod Lincoln." Their humorous original tunes, including "Wine Do Your Stuff," "Seeds and Stems (Again)," and "Lost in the Ozone," put a definitive counterculture stamp on swing music.

Asleep at the Wheel was one of the most popular western swing bands in the 1970s and recorded many well-received albums that revived Bob Wills standards such as "Take Me Back to Tulsa" and "Hubbin' It" for a new generation. The band also created their own original western swing classics, including "Let Me Go Home Whiskey," "Bump Bounce Boogie,"

and "Miles and Miles of Texas." They even played big band classics such as "Choo Choo Ch'Boogie," "Jumpin' at the Woodside," and "Chattanooga Choo Choo" in western swing style. Over the years Asleep at the Wheel has also played and recorded with veterans of the original Texas Playboys such as fiddler Johnny Gimble, electric mandolinist Tiny Moore, and guitarist Eldon Shamblin.

While some of the most talented musicians around played western swing, they never took themselves too seriously. The music and presentation always had a joyous and often humor-

Commander Cody and His Lost Planet Airmen revived western swing for a new generation of listeners.

The western swing band Asleep at the Wheel revisited classic songs by Bob Wills in addition to creating a sound of their own.

ous feel, from Bob Wills hollering out his witty asides, to amusing song titles such as "Boot Scootin' Boogie."

In the 1990s western swing remained popular among those who valued skilled instrumentalists, an insistent dance beat, and a positive musical experience. New swing bands such as Hot Club of Cow-town from Austin have taken the music into the twenty-first century. With its un-canny blend of African American, south-ern cowboy, Mexican, and Cajun sounds cooked up in the hot Texas sun, western swing is music that could only have been invented in the melting pot of the United States.

Chapter Five

Rockabilly Music

Western swing added African American-style blues to its music in the 1930s, '40s, and '50s, while the songs retained their country flavor with fiddles, steel guitars, and cowboy lyrics. In the 1950s a different intermingling of blues and country emerged as a wild new style called rockabilly. While catching the instant attention of a new generation of baby boomers, many who were just reaching their teenage years, it also put a considerable crimp in the careers of traditional honky-tonk singers who had been topping the charts in earlier years. The old-style crooners singing of heartbreak and lovesick blues could not compete with the untamed rockabilly shouters in their gold lamé suits and blue suede shoes.

In a way, rockabilly was the opposite of western swing music, lacking tight arrangements and sophisticated musicianship. While swing bands utilized dozens of virtuoso musicians playing advanced jazz licks, rockabilly groups needed nothing more than a singer accompanied by a stand-up "slap" bass and an electric guitar. Often the guitarist would strum a quick introductory chord, then shout out the first lyrics accappella (with no instrumental backing), before the entire band jumped in with a beat-heavy backup. Kurt Wolff describes the style:

> Given the intense, raw energy the music produced, the simplicity of it all is astounding. At rockabilly's core was the rhythm—a strong and steady beat made with just a guitar and a standup bass played in a slapping style. An electric guitar cut through like a sharp knife, and on top of it all was a hillbilly hepcat singer packing a punkish attitude and an assortment of lurid yelps, hiccups and raspy cries—not to mention swaggering dance moves—that gave the music the threat of danger, that made it sexy. There were no

drums, at least at first, but the use of echo in the studio gave it a beefier illusion. As the music caught on, all sorts of instruments would be added, most commonly saxophone and piano, but at the core always were the two guitars and standup bass—simple, raw and rootsy. It was easy enough for any kid with a guitar, a sneer and an itchy hipbone to at least give it a try.[44]

Hillbilly Boogie

Rockabilly and rock and roll are twins born out of the fusion of country and blues in the late 1940s. At that time honky-tonk artists such as Hank Williams sometimes played what was called "hillbilly boogie" influenced by African American boogie-woogie, popular on what were called "race records," mostly sold in black neighborhoods.

The beat of hillbilly boogie was simple. And it lacked a backbeat, that is, a loud rhythmic beat occurring on the offbeats, a rhythm that originated with black gospel music.

In 1947 African American rhythm and blues (R&B) singer Wynonie Harris reached black and white audiences alike with "Good Rockin' Tonight," credited as one of the first rock-and-roll songs. So that the listener could not fail to hear the exciting beat, the song features hand clapping on the backbeat, behind Harris's vociferous vocals. As the bassist slaps the strings, a rolling "barrelhouse" pianist pounds out

rhythm and melody with his right hand mimicking horn lines while the left hand plays bass lines at the bottom end of the keyboard. The "Wynonie Harris" website describes the song with its suggestive lyrics:

> Harris used the gospel element of hand-clapping on the back-beat . . . to emulate the "rocking" rhythm which had been heard in gospel music for many years. The song is basically a parody of gospel music, with mention of a deacon and an elder doing a distinctly different type

Wynonie Harris (far left) combined the beat of hillbilly and the backbeat of gospel to create one of the first rock-and-roll songs.

of "rocking" than gospel preachers would have mentioned. . . . This record is what started the whole "rocking" craze in blues in the late 1940's, which would eventually lead to the greatest musical revolution of all time. This is probably the most important record in the history of rock and roll—without this record, rock and roll probably never would have happened. [45]

Harris went on to score a string of hits in the late 1940s and early '50s, many with humorous or suggestive titles such as "Sittin' on It All the Time," "I Like My Baby's Pudding," and "Bloodshot Eyes."

The success of this untamed new music did not go unnoticed in the country community. Alabama native Hardrock Gunter was one of the first country-western acts to record with a solid backbeat, and his songs such as 1949's "Birmingham Bounce" featured brisk rockabilly bass rhythms combined with western swing fiddle licks. The song went to number one on the *Billboard* magazine charts and inspired other country acts to step up the tempo and compose lyrics about rockin', rollin', dancin', and jumpin' all night.

Rockin' Round the Clock

Seizing on the music's popularity in 1951, Bill Haley, a northern country performer from Philadelphia, began opening his evening set with a number called "Rock the Joint." Haley had been riding the cowboy bandwagon since the late '40s, singing Jimmie Rodgers's yodels, ballads, and western swing numbers with his two bands, the Four Aces of Western Swing and the Saddlemen.

People immediately took notice when the rapid-fire staccato guitar kicked off the ultimately danceable "Rock the Joint," and soon Haley was in the studio recording "Rocket 88," a tune with a similar beat. The song features a rollicking boogie-woogie piano, shouted vocals, and dueling electric and steel guitars. The song, however, was a few years ahead of its time and did not sell.

In 1952 Haley went back to the Saddlemen and tried to capitalize on the popularity of Hank Williams's song "Cold Cold Heart" by recording a knockoff called "Icy Heart." Haley backed the single with the previously recorded "Rock the Joint." Disc jockeys began playing the B side instead of the honky-tonk number, and "Rock the Joint" was a hit. But, as Robert Oermann writes:

This posed a problem: Black audiences were disappointed that Haley was white, and the mom-and-pop country audience wasn't all that receptive [to the rockabilly sound]. The listening audience that was wild about "Rock the Joint" was a consumer group no one had previously addressed, teenagers. The boots and spurs would have to go. The Saddlemen added a sax player, put on matching tuxedos, and became The Comets. [46]

Wynonie's Blueprint for Rock

On the RollingStone.com web-site, Bill Dahl details the career of Wynonie Harris, the 1940s rhythm and blues (R&B) singer who inspired countless rock and rockabilly artists:

No blues shouter embodied the rollicking good times that he sang of quite like raucous shouter Wynonie Harris. "Mr. Blues," as he was not-so-humbly known, joyously related risqué tales of sex, booze, and endless parties in his trademark raspy voice over some of the jumpingest horn-powered combos of the post-war era. Those wanton ways eventually caught up with Harris, but not before he scored a raft of R&B smashes from 1946 to 1952. Harris was already a sea-soned dancer, drummer, and singer when he left Omaha for L.A. in 1940. . . . Harris joined the star-studded roster of Cincinnati's King Records in 1947. There his sales really soared. Few records made a stronger seismic impact than Harris's 1948 chart-topper "Good Rockin' Tonight.". . . With Hal "Cornbread" Singer on wailing tenor sax and a rocking, socking backbeat, the record provided an easily followed blueprint for the imminent rise of rock & roll a few years later (and gave Elvis Presley some-thing to place on the A side of his second Sun single). After that, Harris was rarely absent from the R&B charts for the next four years, his offerings growing more boldly suggestive all the time. "Grandma Plays the Numbers," "All She Wants to Do Is Rock,". . . [and] "Good Morn-ing Judge" . . . were only a por-tion of the ribald hits Harris scored into 1952 (13 in all)— and then his personal hit parade stopped dead. It certainly wasn't Harris's fault . . . but changing tastes among fickle consumers that accelerated Wynonie Har-ris's sobering fall from favor. . . . Throat cancer silenced him for good in 1969, ending the life of a bigger-than-life R&B pio-neer whose ego matched his tremendous talent.

Bill Haley and His Comets attracted a large teenage audience with their rockabilly music.

When Bill Haley and His Comets released "Crazy Man Crazy" in 1953, it became one of the first rockabilly hits. Haley had another hit the next year with "Shake, Rattle, and Roll." In these songs Haley took the African-inspired beat of rhythm and blues, and stripped away the sexual lyrics, harmonious backing, and blues inflection in the singing. Then he added slick guitar work and other effects from hillbilly music.

In 1954 Haley's success continued when he recorded "Rock Around the Clock," which was played the next year over the opening credits of *The Blackboard Jungle,* a movie about a high school teacher confronted by violent students. "Rock Around the Clock" created a nationwide sensation when overexcited teens caused riots in some theaters. Haley's song shot to number one, and the rock era had begun. By the summer of 1955, the record had sold 1 million copies; by 2001 that number would climb to an astronomical 25 million copies, making it one of the top-selling songs in history. But musical historians continue to debate whether or not Haley's brand of music was truly rockabilly, as Craig Morrison writes in *Go Cat Go!:*

Haley projected the image of a cheerful, optimistic, uncomplicated, unerotic, almost quaint older person having good clean fun at a party. His music was, on the surface, rockabilly: a rhythmic mixing of country music with elements from black music. What, then, does rockabilly have that [Haley's] music does not? In a word, rebellion. In addition, besides having a more personal and intense delivery, rockabilly has a more integrated mixture of black and white styles, the kind of intertwining that comes from direct contact within the community, more common to the South, and not just from paring down western swing and adding rhythms heard on R&B records. Of course, some rockabilly was made by people who had little or no personal contact with black musicians, but they were influenced by rockabillies who did. [47]

Sun Shines over Memphis

The unassuming Haley laid the foundations for the rock-and-roll revolution and went on to become the first—if unlikely—rock superstar. Meanwhile, rockabilly continued on its own path aided by independent record producer Sam Phillips, who operated the Memphis Recording Service in Tennessee. And while Haley lacked the outlaw attitude, the rockabilly mob in Memphis—including Elvis Presley, Johnny Cash, and Jerry Lee Lewis—were some of the craziest boys in the business.

Phillips's record business was housed in an unassuming little storefront on Union Avenue in Memphis, a town where blues, hillbilly, bluegrass, and honky-tonk musicians converged hoping to find fame and fortune. And Phillips was one of the best recording engineers around in the early 1950s. With primitive recording equipment (by today's standards), Phillips managed to improve the sound of records by experimenting with tone and balance, mixing the final product on tiny speakers that were similar to those found in automobile dashboards. To achieve the echo and reverb sounds found in cavernous concert halls, the producer recorded his singers in a concrete stairwell.

Although Phillips's business card read "We record anything—anywhere—anytime," [48] the record engineer did not need to advertise—Memphis Recording Service was the best studio in town. And in his search for new sounds, its sympathetic owner auditioned just about any musician who came through the door.

Today the talent who first auditioned at Memphis Recording Service reads like a who's who of blues superstars. Phillips worked with the then-unknown B.B. King, Little Milton, Howling Wolf, Ike Turner, and others. After Bill Haley had a hit imitating Ike Turner's version of "Rocket 88," Phillips changed the name of his business to Sun Studios.

Elvis "the Hillbilly Cat" Presley

Although Phillips was recording men who would become blues legends, due to prejudicial '50s attitudes, white-owned radio stations refused to play records by black musicians, and white store owners would not sell them. Naturally, Phillips was continually looking for a white singer who could pack the emotional punch routinely delivered by black artists. As his partner Marion Keisker said, "I recall that Sam had said, several times, that he wished he could find a white singer with the soul and feeling and the kind of voice to do what was then identified as rhythm & blues songs."[49] Phillips's wish came true in 1953 when a truck driver from Tupelo, Mississippi, came to the studio to make a demo record.

At that time Elvis Presley, whose family had recently moved to Memphis, was just another poor country boy with a dream. But Phillips recognized a certain quality in Presley's voice. Keisker described it, saying, "I felt the hair on the back of my neck begin to prickle in some way."[50] Phillips teamed Presley with Scotty Black on guitar and Bill Black on bass. Both men had extensive experience playing country music. Presley boomed out a raved-up rockabilly version of blues singer Arthur "Big Boy" Crudup's "That's All Right," and a legend was born.

In 1955 Presley recorded several rockabilly singles including "Baby Let's Play House" and "Mystery Train," which became hits on country charts. And billed as a country artist, "the Hillbilly Cat," by Phillips, Presley appeared on the *Grand Ole Opry* and on a similar show, *Louisiana Hayride,*

where he became a cast member for a year and a half.

Presley's first singles sold fairly well in Memphis, and Phillips booked him on the country circuit with *Opry* stars such as Faron Young and the Carter Sisters. When Presley came onstage, however, his hip-shaking delivery, shockingly long sideburns, and bad-boy attitude traumatized parents—and made teenage girls swoon.

A young Elvis Presley changed the face of country music by adding provocative moves to his onstage act.

Uncharted Musical Waters

When rockabilly first achieved widespread popularity, music industry officials did not know how to categorize it, since rock and roll was not yet an accepted style and the sound was not really country. This controversy is discussed in the Country Music Foundation's Country: The Music and Musicians:

When Memphis DJ Dewey Philips played Elvis Presley's "That's All Right" and "Blue Moon of Kentucky" for the first time and then interviewed the nineteen-year-old over the air, station WHBQ received fourteen telegrams and forty-seven phone calls for the local boy. Most were from new fans—but not everyone took an immediate liking to Elvis's sound. And as Presley's records began to gain a foothold on regional country charts in Memphis, New Orleans, and Dallas, the muttering in the country music industry began: *It's not country, it's Negro music. It's pop. It's something, but it's not country.*

The protests only became more heated as Elvis and the rockabillies that followed him proved to be the hottest thing going on the country charts. Paul Ackerman, former music editor for *Billboard,* stated in no

Elvis's rockabilly sound was not universally liked.

uncertain terms in a 1958 article for *High Fidelity* that "well-entrenched artists, talent managers and other members of the trade resented him [Elvis] fiercely. One day I had two phone calls from music executives in Nashville, Tennessee. Both demanded that *Billboard* remove Presley from the best-selling country chart on the ground that—so they said—he was not truly representative of the country field.". . .

Through all the commotion in the industry, country fans simply bought the records, wrote and called their radio stations, and kept putting nickels in the jukebox. Elvis and the boys were making some of the best [music] ever heard.

Presley quickly became superstar material, and in 1955 Phillips sold his contract to RCA for little more than $35,000, a sum the producer used to promote other rockabilly acts.

"Blue Suede Shoes," "the Killer," and Twitty

At RCA Presley left rockabilly behind to make pop records—and rock history. Meanwhile, Phillips began to develop a stable of rockabilly artists who were flocking to his studio hoping to become the next Elvis. Although none achieved quite the same level of fame, musicians such as Carl Perkins, Jerry Lee Lewis, and Johnny Cash have gone on to become legends in their own right.

Perkins, born into poverty in Tiptonville, Tennessee, in 1932, scored a major hit in 1956 with the now-classic rockabilly anthem "Blue Suede Shoes," which simultaneously landed on the top of the country, pop, and R&B charts. Perkins was seriously injured in a car accident soon after, and Presley scored his own hit with "Blue Suede Shoes."

Although his career floundered, Perkins's rockabilly originals such as "Everybody's Trying to Be My Baby" and "Honey Don't" were revived in the mid-1960s by the Beatles.

Meanwhile, Jerry Lee Lewis—one of the most outrageous, piano-pounding showstoppers in rockabilly history—was signed to Sun Records by Phillips. Lewis, who grew up in a strict, religious family in Ferriday, Louisiana, first recorded as a country artist, singing the classic "Crazy Arms" in

1956. But Lewis left his roots behind in 1957 when he recorded the delirious "Good Rockin' Tonight" and "Great Balls of Fire."

Parents who were hoping Elvis Presley's version of rockabilly would soon fade away were scandalized when wild-man Lewis, known as "the Killer," performed in a leopard-skin jacket with his long blond hair flapping in his face. Teenagers in the audience screamed, yelled, and tore up the seats in the auditorium. And Lewis's physical abuse of his pianos was legendary. He danced on top, played the upper keys with the heels of his shoes, and more. As Lewis stated: "One night I just filled a Coca-Cola bottle with gasoline and took it [onstage] with me. . . . When I got through doing 'Great Balls of Fire,' I sprinkled some of the gasoline inside the piano and threw a match in. I never could believe a piano could burn like that, but it did."[51]

When Lewis married his thirteen-year-old cousin in 1958, his career burned out as fast as his gasoline-soaked piano. But there were other country singers whose musical stars were on the rise. Mississippi native Conway Twitty (whose real name was Harold Jenkins) sounded so much like Presley that Phillips did not even bother to release his records, believing that the public was not yet ready for an Elvis imitator. Twitty wrote a rockabilly song "Rockhouse" that was recorded by Roy Orbison. While Orbison went on to rock-and-roll stardom with hits such as "Only the Lonely" and "Oh Pretty

Jerry Lee Lewis's manic performances and pounding piano were a hit with young audiences.

Woman," Twitty returned to his country roots, in the following decades charting fifty-five number one country hits—more than any other singer in history. Meanwhile, Johnny Cash, another singer who would become a country icon, recorded a few rockabilly sides for Phillips.

Dark and Light Sides of Rockabilly

The hit records made in Memphis inspired other producers to seek out their own rockabilly acts. Down the road in Nashville, Gene Vincent laid down the tracks for the classic "Be-Bop-a-Lula" in 1956. Originally hired by Capitol Records to compete with Elvis, Vincent was a talented songwriter who had started out—like so many others— singing country. But he took to the rockabilly image with an uncommon passion.

Dressed entirely in black leather, with his hair greased back, his mouth twisted into a sneer, and a permanent limp from a motorcycle accident, Vincent's bad-boy look rivaled that of Presley, Lewis, or any other rockabilly artist. Backed by nimble-fingered guitarist Cliff Gallup's lightning-fast, quick-picked guitar licks, Vincent's raw, untamed sound on songs such as "Race with the Devil," "Crazy Legs," and "Bluejean Bop" defined late '50s rockabilly. Robert Palmer writes about Vincent's innovative style and tragic demise:

> He was the rockabilly who first wore black leather, the costume of choice for rockers for generations afterward. He developed the biker

image and menacing stage swagger that are still imitated today. He anticipated punk rock with his thrashing moves, leaps from amplifiers, and writhing on stage floors. He was also among the first to take the rock 'n' roll revolution overseas.

The alcohol and pill consumption that fueled his mood swings and violent outbursts was notorious. Vincent's dark, erratic behavior drove crowds wild but alienated the music business. Tormented all his life by a leg that had never healed properly following a mo-

Gene Vincent's black leather outfits and bad boy sensibilities gave rise to a rock-and-roll image that would be embraced by musicians for years to come.

torcycle accident, he died of hemorrhaged stomach ulcers at the age of thirty-six.[52]

Vincent's tough-guy image was sharply contrasted with the clean-cut Buddy Holly, whose trademark thick-framed glasses, skinny ties, and suit coats made him look more like a college professor than one of rockabilly's most talented singer-songwriters.

Holly began his career in his hometown of Lubbock, Texas, playing radio gigs with a friend booked as Buddy & Bob—Western and Bop. After hearing Elvis, Holly formed the Crickets and wrote a slew of instant classics such as "That'll Be the Day," "Maybe Baby," "Rave On," and "Peggy Sue."

The End of Rockabilly

When Buddy Holly died in a small plane crash in Iowa on February 3, 1959, it signaled the end of an era. Like many other musical styles, rockabilly's lifespan was like the two-minute songs it produced—short, sweet, and often rough. At the time of Holly's death, the founders of rockabilly were no longer playing that style. Carl Perkins was recuperating from a serious car accident, Elvis had been drafted into the army, Jerry Lee Lewis was hounded into (temporary) oblivion by his marriage to his cousin, and Conway Twitty had become a teen idol, joining the ranks of sugary crooners such as Fabian, Pat Boone, Paul Anka, and others.

The rebellious music of the '50s, was quickly drowned out in the 1960s by the Beatles, who were, ironically, heavily influenced by Presley, Vincent, Holly, and other rockabilly artists. During the 1970s, however, the style experienced a revival, especially in Europe, where old rockabilly records were reissued in Great Britain, Germany, Holland, and elsewhere. Artists such as Carl Perkins, who had been living in semiobscurity, were suddenly in hot demand on the European concert circuit.

The fad soon traveled back across the Atlantic, and American groups such as the Stray Cats sold millions of records blasting out the sounds of rockabilly.

In the '80s and '90s, the raw energy and rebellious attitudes of rockabilly endeared itself to punk rockers, who created "psychobilly," taking musical insubordination to a new level of madness. Performers such as the Cramps, the Reverend Horton Heat, and Mojo Nixon owed a great debt to rockabilly rhythms even as they filled out their CDs with irreverent parodies of the real thing. Meanwhile, the Blasters and the "Rockabilly Filly" Rosie Flores gained followings by presenting a more authentic vision of rockabilly.

In the twenty-first century on any given night rockabilly is played in thousands of bars across the world. Fans of the style can see live bands whose look and sound bring back the rockabilly glory days of the '50s. From the hillbilly boogie of the 1940s, three chords and an attitude spawned rockabilly madness, and the world will never be the same.

Chapter Six

The Nashville Hit Makers

In the later half of the 1950s, rockabilly and rock and roll severely affected the country music industry, stealing a majority of its formerly loyal fans in a few short years. This was seen most dramatically at the Ryman Auditorium where the *Grand Ole Opry* was held every Saturday night. From the mid-1920s until 1954, the show was sold out nearly every weekend. By 1958 the auditorium was half empty—or worse—at show time. And as steel player Joe Talbot states, it was rock and roll that hurt the *Opry:*

> I really hate to admit this now, but I hated rock 'n' roll because it killed country music. . . . I mean, it just wiped it out. The audience liked the dance beat, the humor, the energy, the simplicity, the excitement of Elvis Presley. These people put on tremendous shows. I think that's one of the big things that caused our audience to move to rock 'n' roll, because all we had

to do was stand up there and sing ten hit songs and sign autographs. These people put on a real show. That's why temporarily we lost our market to rock 'n' roll.[53]

The popularity of live country music was also on the wane on national radio programs. In 1957 NBC canceled the *Grand Ole Opry* radio show, and in 1960 Chicago's WLS dropped the *National Barn Dance*. Both were forced to struggle along on local stations.

Changes in radio affected country music in other ways. After World War II, radio stations began to proliferate. But instead of each station tailoring its format to local listeners from a wide range of music, station managers began to program a new concept called "top forty," in which the same songs were played over and over. Songs were pulled from the forty best-selling records across America, and by the late '50s that meant rock and roll.

While there were a few country artists, such as Johnny Cash, who crossed over to the pop charts, top forty was a disaster for country music. By 1960 there were only eighty-one country stations in the entire United States, where thousands of top forty stations filled the radio dials. In addition, television, which was practically nonexistent in the early '50s, prompted people to abandon radio in droves by the end of the decade. It was hard times in the country music industry, and musicians and executives were desperate to regain their former fortunes.

Nashville Goes Modern

In 1958 country music executives formed the Country Music Association (CMA) to promote the financial interests of their industry. That meant getting more country radio stations on the air and convincing advertisers that the millions of people who were still "country" were an important segment of the buying public. The old-time, bluegrass, and honky-tonk music that had made earlier country so successful was no longer fashionable. A consultant for the CMA issued a memo that outlined the organization's stance:

In its heyday, the Grand Ole Opry *would attract a full house with performances by artists such as Patsy Cline.*

"*Modern* country music has no relationship to rural or mountain life. It is the music of this *Nation,* of this country, the music of the people. You find no screech fiddles, no twangy guitars, no mournful nasal twangs in the *modern* Nashville sound of country music."[54]

The efforts of the CMA quickly began to pay off, and the number of country radio stations climbed to more than two hundred by 1965. (Today there are more than twenty-five hundred, and country is the most popular radio format in America.) The CMA also grabbed the public's attention when it opened the Country Music Hall of Fame and instituted the Country Music Awards in 1967.

The Nashville Sound

With millions of dollars at stake, the CMA did its part to promote country in the United States. And to rid country of "screech fiddles" and "twangy guitars," producers in Nashville began to "sweeten" the sound of country, hoping to make it more palatable to average Americans, who by now lived in suburban homes, not mountain cabins.

Several record producers have been credited with softening country's rougher sounds, including Owen Bradley, Don Law, and guitarist extraordinaire Chet Atkins. These men muted the steel guitar, banned fiddle breaks and nasal hillbilly singing, and added gospel-like background choruses, lush string arrangements provided by the Nashville Symphony, and velvety, sweet lead vocals of syrupy country crooners like Ferlin Husky, Faron Young, Marty Robbins, Jim Reeves, and Eddy Arnold. The sound they produced was described by a 1962 trade magazine as having a "relaxed, tensionless feeling and loose, easygoing beat."[55]

The new brand of country music was known as "country-pop," "countrypolitan," or the "Nashville Sound." Each song was written by a professional songwriter, handpicked by a producer, and sung by a squeaky-clean vocalist whose public image represented wholesome country values. The backing music was played by an exclusive group of talented session musicians, who appeared, often uncredited, on literally thousands of records. The basic countrypolitan session band of the 1960s consisted of Grady Martin on guitar, Roy Huskey Jr. on bass, Floyd Cramer or Hargus "Pig" Robbins on piano, Charlie McCoy on harmonica, and Buddy Harmon on drums. As Kurt Wolff writes:

They were consummate professionals, and their licks, fills, and rhythms frequently gave the songs additional flair—Martin's nylon-string work on Marty Robbins' "El Paso" and Lefty Frizzell's "Saginaw Michigan"; Cramer's slurred piano riffs on Hank Locklin's "Please Help Me I'm Falling." The cream of this crop came to be known as the A Team, and they

Atkins and Bradley

Chet Atkins and Owen Bradley were the chief architects of the Nashville Sound. Kurt Wolff writes about their work in Country Music: The Rough Guide.

Guitarist Atkins and pianist Bradley were the men at ground zero of the Nashville Sound's development. Settling in Nashville in 1950, Atkins played guitar on numerous sessions, recorded as a solo artist for RCA, and in his spare time led a laid-back group at the Carousel Club in a seedy downtown district called Printer's Alley. Many of Music City's future session stalwarts jammed with Atkins at the Carousel, including pianist Floyd Cramer, drummer Buddy Harman, and saxophonist Boots Randolph. Atkins was hired in 1952 . . . at RCA; by 1960 he was head of A&R [artists and repertory], in charge of a roster that included Eddy Arnold, Jim Reeves, and Don Gibson, and would soon take on Waylon Jennings, Charley Pride, and Dolly Parton, among many others.

Bradley worked for years in Nashville as a local bandleader and musical director at WSM radio (home of the *Grand Ole Opry*) before he was hired by Decca to assist producer Paul Cohen. He eventually ran the label's Nashville division. . . . As a producer, Bradley worked with a huge range of artists, including Red Foley, Kitty Wells, Webb Pierce, Bill Anderson, Conway Twitty, Loretta Lynn, and Bill Monroe. His most famous charge, though, was Patsy Cline, whom he turned from a brash honky-tonk wannabe into a smooth, hitmaking country stylist.

Both Bradley and Atkins regularly used background choruses, strings and horns on the country records they produced, ironing the twang out of the arrangements and giving the music an uptown sheen. Along with Arnold, Cline, and Reeves, other artists who successfully straddled this countrypop boundary include the Browns, Sonny James, Jimmy Dean, Marty Robbins, George Hamilton V, and Ferlin Huskie.

shifted frequently between [different record companies].

Finally, there were the Jordanaires and the Anita Kerr Singers, vocal groups who graced the backdrop of countless Nashville recordings. In addition to her singing duties, Kerr worked out the arrangements on numerous recordings and even did some producing for RCA (one of the first and only women allowed to perform such a task). Alongside Bradley and Atkins, she was an integral force in the Nashville Sound's development.[56]

Along with hiring professional musicians, most hit makers in the '60s used a few proven songwriters. Felice and Boudleaux Bryant, a husband-wife team, wrote hits such as "Love Hurts" and "Richest Man in the World" in addition to the Everly Brothers's hits such as "Bye Bye Love" and "Wake Up Little Susie." Cindy Walker penned western swing, honky-tonk, and rockabilly songs in addition to her Nashville Sound hits such as "You Don't Know Me" sung by Eddy Arnold and "Distant Drums," a hit for Jim Reeves. Harlan Howard was another well-known writer of number one records, including "Streets of Baltimore," "Tiger by the Tail," and Patsy Cline's famous "I Fall to Pieces."

Countrypolitan Crooners

While writers, producers, and session musicians labored behind the scenes, the stars of the Nashville Sound were the singers whose faces appeared on the record sleeves and whose names were on the labels.

The first official countrypolitan hit, produced by Atkins, was Don Gibson's 1958 "Oh Lonesome Me"/"I Can't Stop Loving You." The mournful songs were both written by the singer—on the same day—and they have both gone on to become country standards.

"Gentleman" Jim Reeves was another velvet-voiced singer who embodied the Nashville Sound. Born in Texas in 1923, Reeves began his career in 1952 filling in for Hank Williams when the honky-tonk superstar was drunk and failed to appear for a *Louisiana Hayride* gig. In 1959 Reeves scored a major hit with "He'll Have to Go," crooning the lyrics "Put your sweet lips a little closer to the phone, let's pretend we're together all alone"[57] over a muted musical backdrop. During the early 1960s, Reeves dominated the country charts with hits such as "Guilty" and "Welcome to My World."

Reeves loved to fly his own airplane to gigs; when his small plane crashed in 1964, the beloved singer was killed instantly. By dying at the height of his career, however, the singer went on to achieve cult status. He was inducted into the Country Music Hall of Fame in 1967.

While Reeves's career was cut short by tragedy, Porter Wagoner, "the Thin Man from West Plains" (Missouri), had a long and bountiful career. Like so many others who utilized the Nashville

Sound, Wagoner, born in 1927 in the Ozark Mountains, began his career singing honky-tonk. His flamboyant style included outrageous, shimmering Nudie suits, and his blond hair was styled in an inflated pompadour. Wagoner music, however, was more than fluff.

Wagoner's first number one hit, "A Satisfied Mind," made him a national star in 1955, and he was a regular on the *Opry* by 1957. The flashy singer went national with his own TV program, *Porter Wagoner Show,* in 1960, and his brand of corny jokes and country music attracted a wide audience. Wagoner was backed by a pair of what he called "gal singers," Norma Jean and Dolly Parton, both of whom became stars in their own right. Meanwhile, Parton and Wagoner recorded several best-selling albums together, and the beautiful harmonious duets are considered by some to be pure country gold.

Throughout his career Wagoner mixed the straight-ahead honky-tonk style with the Nashville Sound, making sure the strings and choruses did not dilute the true country edge. But the titles of his hit songs—such as "I've Enjoyed as Much of This as I Can Stand," "Cold Dark Waters," "Green, Green Grass of Home," and "The Cold Hard Facts of Life"—demonstrate the sentimentality often found in country-pop.

Dolly Parton's Rags to Riches

When Parton split from Wagoner, the Thin Man from West Plains was deeply

With the velvety voice of Jim Reeves, country music began to lose its "twangy" edge in the early 1960s.

distressed, and the parting was not amicable. Parton, however, was too great a force to be held back.

Today Dolly Parton is as well known for her movies and theme park, Dollywood, as she is for her country music. But from the time she broke into the Nashville music business fresh out of high school, Parton has been recognized for her songwriting talents, singing ability, attractive persona, and sharp business sense.

Charley Pride

Charley Pride is one of the few African Americans playing the Nashville Sound. On the "Charley Pride—First African American Inducted into the Country Music Hall of Fame" website, Damien Allen offers this biographical information about Pride:

Charley Pride has had an illustrious music career. One of music's premiere artists, Pride is country's first African-American star. For the past quarter century, Pride has been one of the Top 15 best-selling artists of all time. His body of work includes a legacy of 36 No. 1 hit singles, over 25 million albums sold worldwide, 31 gold and 4 platinum albums—including one quadruple-platinum.

Charley Pride was elected to the Country Music Hall of Fame in 2000. Election to the Country Music Hall of Fame is the highest honor in country music.

Charley Frank Pride was born in Sledge, Mississippi, on March 18, 1938. Charlie's parents were both sharecroppers and cotton pickers. . . . Charley grew up listening to country music. He walked around the house singing songs of Hank Williams and Roy Acuff. At the age of six, his happiest moments were spent listening to the Grand Ole Opry on the country music radio station. . . . When Charlie Pride was fourteen, he bought his first guitar from Sears and Roebuck and taught himself how to play by listening to different songs on the radio. . . .

By 1966 Charlie had recorded thirteen songs and was made best country and western male vocalist. . . . Pride has topped the charts over the years with songs that now stand as modern classics. "Kiss an Angel Good Morning" went on to be a million-selling crossover single. Other memorable hits include "Is Anybody Goin' to San Antone?," "I'm So Afraid of Losing You Again," "Mississippi Cotton Picking Delta Town,". . . "When I Stop Leaving I'll Be Gone,". . . "Mountain of Love," and "You're So Good When You're Bad," to name a few.

Dolly Parton used her dirt-poor childhood and female perspective as material for many of her songs.

Parton, born in 1946, has true country roots, and her early life sounds like an old-time song. She was the eighth of twelve children born to a poverty-stricken couple in a cabin in the Smoky Mountains of Tennessee. Like so many others, she was inspired by the music she heard in church—and played with her extended family.

An uncle took Parton to Nashville, where she recorded an original song, "Puppy Love," when she was only fourteen. By the time she graduated from high school in 1964, she was writing hit songs for other artists. In 1967 Parton began to write songs that showed a strong, feminist side that was not found in any style of music before the mid-1970s. Wolff describes the ironically titled song "Dumb Blonde" as "a take-no-punches song about smashing sexist stereotypes. Like other songs soon to come ('Just Because I'm a Woman' [and] 'When Possession Gets Too Strong') . . . it revealed a young woman unafraid to put forward a strong female perspective."[58]

Parton also painted a realistic picture of her dirt-poor childhood and the hardships she overcame in songs such as "Coat of Many Colors," "To Daddy," and "In the Good Old Days (When Times Were Bad)." By the late '70s, Parton had transcended the role of country music singer to become a movie star and a superstar with a broad mainstream fan base.

Other Women of Nashville

Loretta Lynn was another woman of country music who used autobiographical material to write hit songs. Like Parton, Lynn's life was one of struggle and hardship followed by fame and fortune. Born in 1935 in isolated Butcher Holler, Kentucky, Loretta Webb's father struggled to survive, laboring for little pay in local coal mines.

Loretta was only thirteen when she married Oliver Lynn Jr. By the time she was eighteen the couple had four children. Despite her stormy marriage, Lynn aspired to become a singing star. In 1960 she recorded her first single, "I'm a Honky Tonk Girl," and after that her career took off.

Lynn continued to write songs about her life and the world around her. In addition to honky-tonks and coal mines, the country star has penned songs about drunk, cheating husbands, back-stabbing women, and even birth control pills. Songs such as "Don't Come Home a Drinkin' (with Lovin' on Your Mind)," "Who's Gonna Take the Garbage Out," and "Your Squaw Is on the Warpath" sum up the rough and tough attitudes of this country star. Wolff writes about the reasons for Lynn's popularity:

Men as well as women identified with Lynn's songs not only because of the strong, clear vocals, but also because of their honesty. Although committed to her marriage, she was never afraid to speak of its troubles and pains. Fed-up housewives heard "Don't Come Home A Drinkin" and made it the first of her many #1 hits. Other songs such as "Dear Uncle Sam" (an anti-Vietnam War song from the point of view of a suffering wife), "Wings Upon Your Horns" (where an "angel" girl is seduced by a "devil" man), and, of course, "The Pill" challenged society's sexual and political boundaries. [59]

By the mid-1960s Lynn was topping the country charts with regularity and was a member of the *Grand Ole Opry*. In 1970 she wrote the autobiographical song "Coal Miner's Daughter." In 1976 Lynn wrote an autobiography of the same name, and that was made into a movie starring Sissy Spacek in 1980.

Loretta Lynn and Dolly Parton have provided inspiration to countless female country singers who grew up listening to their music. But they were not the only female stars of Nashville in the '50s and '60s. Skeeter Davis, Dottie West, Connie Smith, Jeannie C. Riley, and others recorded many successful records utilizing the Nashville Sound.

Loretta Lynn holds her lifetime achievement award at the 1985 American Music Awards. She inspired many female country singers over the years.

Epic Ballads and Saga Songs

Countrypolitan was not the only noise emanating from Nashville in the late '50s—although it dominated the charts. At that time there was a college folk music revival, and that fad provided a market for a new type of country music based on the old-time historical ballads. Known as "saga" or "epic" music, these songs combined up-tempo beats and slick arrangements with adventure stories.

In 1959 Johnny Horton chalked up the first of these hits with "The Battle of New Orleans," based on the unlikely topic of Andrew Jackson's army beating the British in the War of 1812. Horton followed up with several crossover epic hits, including "North to Alaska," "Sink the *Bismarck,*" and "When It's Springtime in Alaska," before his untimely death in a 1960 car accident.

Horton's success inspired Marty Robbins to write "El Paso," a ten-verse number about a cowboy who shoots a rival in a Texas bar because he made a pass at the beautiful dancer Felina. Robbins later recorded dozens of cowboy and gunfighter ballads, including "Big Iron," "The Little Green Valley," and "Saddle Tramp." Other notable Nashville ballads include Jimmy Dean's "Big Bad John," Jim Reeves's "The Blizzard," and Eddy Arnold's "Tennessee Stud."

Nashville Novelties

The saga songs of the early '60s were an anomaly in an era dominated by the

Roger Miller found country music success with a string of hit novelty songs.

sugary Nashville Sound, and by 1964 the fad for historical ballads was over. The public remained hungry for novelty songs, however, and singer-songwriter Roger Miller was there to provide.

In the 1950s, like hundreds of others, Miller was what he describes as "a young ambitious songwriter, walking the streets of Nashville, trying to get anybody and everybody to record my songs."[60] By the 1960s he had found small success writing songs for George Jones, Faron Young, and others. He even recorded several minor hits, including "You Don't Want My Love" and "When Two Worlds Collide," on his own.

Hee Haw

In 1969 CBS began airing the TV program Hee Haw. *What the* Grand Ole Opry *was to country radio,* Hee Haw *was to country television—not surprising, since the two programs shared a group of writers and performers. Although the show was filmed in Hollywood, almost every hit maker from Nashville appeared on* Hee Haw, *and it was an integral part of the country music business during its long run. The following information is provided on "A Little About Hee Haw," the* Hee Haw *tribute website:*

"Hee Haw" premiered on CBS on June 15, 1969. Hosted by popular country performers Buck Owens and Roy Clark, the show was a country alternative to "Laugh-In." The corny jokes were delivered, naturally, in a cornfield. "Hee Haw" enjoyed success on CBS for only one year before falling victim to a network purging of all things country. Shows like "The Beverly Hillbillies," "The Jim Nabors Show," and "Green Acres" were taken off the air as CBS tried to distance itself from its rural image. The show's producers got the last laugh, though, as the show ran for an amazing 25 seasons before production ceased in 1993.

The show began with incredible comedy writers such as Archie Campbell, Don Herron, and Gordie Tapp, who . . . were also successful on screen, playing such lovable characters as the old doctor . . . the radio announcer (for station KORN) . . . [and] the storekeeper plagued by a bumbling clerk. "Hee Haw" was known for its down-home, simple humor, which appealed to people all over the world.

The humor may have been homespun and geared to the lowest common denominator, but the music was first-class. Buck Owens' award-winning Buckaroos provided much of the musical entertainment. Musical guests included all the big name entertainers of the day, from Loretta Lynn and Charley Pride to Garth Brooks and Alan Jackson.

Country musician Buck Owens and the Hee Haw *cast.*

Money was scarce, however, so Miller decided to record a few of his novelty songs for the Mercury label in 1964. Miller was shocked when "Dang Me" went to number one on the country charts before crossing over to become a pop hit. This surprising success was followed by "Chug-a-Lug," "Do Wacka-Do," and his anthem, "King of the Road." Miller's success netted him five Grammy Awards in 1965, and six more the following year. Wolff describes the key to Miller's success in an era when the Beatles had absolute domination over the pop charts: "[Miller] magically mixed tight, spare arrangements with a hot-fired country spirit, insanely clever wordplay, and a totally wacked-out sense of humor. His songs didn't always make sense (My Uncle Used to Love Me But She Died), but that was part of their beauty."[61]

Miller wasn't the only Nashville singer to ride to the top on the novelty song. David Dudley was a truck-driving man, and his songs were wildly popular with big-rig drivers. Dudley's most famous tune is "Six Days on the Road," a truck-driving anthem covered by everyone from blues artist Taj Mahal to country rockers the Flying Burrito Brothers. In 1968 Bill Malone described Dudley's singing style, writing, "In many songs, Dudley affects a hard-driving, virile style of singing replete with mumbles and slurred expressions which make him sound like an adult Elvis Presley."[62]

Whether or not Dudley was inspired by Elvis, his chart-topping songs in the '60s and '70s cemented the link between trucks, country music, and Nashville. A sampling of the titles—such as "Truck Drivin' Son-of-a-Gun," "There Ain't No Easy Run," "Trucker's Prayer," "Me and Ole C.B.," and "Rolaids, Doan's Pills, and Preparation H"—reflect the serious as well as the humorous aspects of propelling an eighteen-wheeler down the road.

Music City U.S.A.

Whether releasing songs about semis chugging down the road or heartbroken ditties filled with luxuriant string arrangements, in the 1960s Nashville easily earned its nickname "Music City U.S.A." And it has retained that title ever since. Today Nashville attracts thousands of hopeful singers, songwriters, and musicians to its famed "Music Row" every year. All major record labels have offices in Nashville, and dozens of million-selling hits emanate from that city. From its humble musical beginnings as the hometown of the *Grand Ole Opry,* Music City U.S.A. has grown to become the creative and financial heart and soul of the country music business.

Chapter Seven

New Sounds, New Fans

Nashville producers and record executives have dominated the country music business since the late 1950s. And while the recording establishment has remained firmly entrenched in Music City U.S.A., occasionally events beyond its control have shaped and shifted the direction of the country style. While some of these changes, such as "outlaw" music, were first resisted by executives, they were embraced by fans, and country music continued to gain popularity among the general public. The growth of the industry has been phenomenal over the past several decades, and country music is more popular than ever. But it was often musicians from outside the country music establishment who helped validate the style as true American music.

Country Rock

In the later part of the 1960s, while Nashville was, ironically, distancing itself from its traditional roots, best-selling rock-and-roll musicians began to adapt

the sounds of bluegrass and honky-tonk. And because of their huge popularity among the masses, these rock superstars helped create a new audience for country music.

Hardly anyone was bigger than Bob Dylan in the 1960s, having influenced a generation of rock bands to explore personal, poetic musical themes based on folk music. In 1965 Bob Dylan "went electric," picking up a Fender Stratocaster, thereby instantly inventing "folk rock."

Over the next several years, Dylan's folk rock evolved into country rock on albums such as 1967's *John Wesley Harding,* which combines Dylan's trademark storytelling lyrics with simple old-time country music backing. The follow-up to that album, *Nashville Skyline,* features country arrangements on songs such as "Lay Lady Lay" that include pedal steel and flat-picking guitar played by some of Nashville's finest studio musicians. Dylan even generated controversy when he sang a duet on "Girl from the North Country" with Johnny Cash. At the height of the Vietnam War era, some of Dylan's counterculture fans disapproved of him singing with Cash, who represented the political establishment.

While some complained about Dylan's new direction, the innovative superstar generated his usual army of imitators. In 1968 the Byrds—a rock band that had previous hits with Dylan songs such as "Mr. Tambourine Man"— released a country rock record *Sweetheart of the Rodeo*. This album, also recorded in Nashville, features banjos, pedal steels, and mandolins playing true-to-style bluegrass and honky-tonk

By combining country, folk, and rock, counterculture musicians like Bob Dylan attracted new fans to country music.

arrangements. In addition to covering country standards such as "I Am a Pilgrim" and "You Don't Miss Your Water," the Byrds played original country rock songs written by eighteen-year-old Gram Parsons, who had recently joined the group.

American Cosmic Music

Parsons was a leading proponent of country rock, a term he disliked, preferring instead "American cosmic music."[63] Parsons left the Byrds, however, after *Sweetheart of the Rodeo,* and along with Byrds's bassist and mandolin player, Chris Hillman, went on to found the Flying Burrito Brothers, another extremely influential country rock group. Soon Parsons moved on again, spending time with the Rolling Stones, inspiring that British rock group to write country-flavored numbers such as "Honky Tonk Woman," "Country Honk," "Dead Flowers," and "Wild Horses."

Parsons released two well-received solo albums—*GP* and *Return of the Grievous Angel*—in the early '70s. He was backed by members of Elvis Presley's band, many of whom had deep country roots. Parsons also discovered Emmylou Harris singing in a bar, and her soaring ethereal harmonies can be heard on Parson's solo albums. Harris went on to become a star herself, mixing bluegrass, rock, honky-tonk, and swing styles on her critically acclaimed albums.

Parsons died of a drug overdose in 1973 at the age of twenty-six, but his influence was widely felt, as the "Gram Parsons" website states:

Gram Parsons (second from right), pictured here with his group The Flying Burrito Brothers, *was one of the founding fathers of country rock.*

The long list of musicians Gram Parson influenced includes but is not limited to Elvis Costello, U2, Rodney Crowell, Dave Edmunds, The Jayhawks, Marty Stuart, Black Crowes, The Lemonheads, Nick Lowe, Uncle Tupelo, Son Volt, Tom Petty, The Eagles, The Rolling Stones and of course, Emmylou Harris, who carried his musical vision to fruition and beyond.[64]

Country Outlaws

The longhaired hippie superstars fueled their music with tequila, marijuana, cocaine, and other drugs. But they were not the only country music rebels of the mid-1970s. In fact, an entire genre, known as "outlaw," came to dominate the country music charts throughout the decade. (The term itself originated in a 1972 Lee Clayton song "Ladies Love Outlaws" recorded by Waylon Jennings and released on an album of the same name.) The leading outlaws, such as Jennings, Willie Nelson, David Allan Coe, Kris Kristofferson, and others, were determined to rebel against the syrupy-sweet Nashville Sound that had come to dominate the country charts at that time. As Kurt Wolff writes:

Much of the power in this Nashville Sound system lay in the hands of the producers. They picked the songs, assigned the session musicians, and

Gram Parsons, the Grievous Angel

Gram Parsons was one of the founding fathers of country rock, as Joe Hauler writes in his "Gram Parsons Biography" on Rolling Stone.com:

Born Ingram Cecil Connor in Winter Haven, Fla. on November 5, 1946, Gram Parsons is generally regarded as one of the pioneers of the country-rock genre. Seamlessly blending straight-ahead acoustic rock with the bluesy honky-tonk of country, Parsons' groundbreaking style, which he called "Cosmic American Music," ultimately influenced acts like the Eagles and the Rolling Stones.

The grandson of a wealthy agriculturist, Parsons learned to play piano at age nine after seeing Elvis Presley perform at his school auditorium. . . . [In 1968] Parsons met Chris Hillman, bassist for the Byrds, who was so impressed with the young musician that he . . . asked him to join the band. Parsons had an immediate impact on the songwriting of the Byrds and spearheaded the country influenced *Sweetheart of the Rodeo*. Parsons' stint in the Byrds lasted just three months, however. . . .

Along with Hillman, who also quit the Byrds, Parsons formed the Flying Burrito Brothers. The duo released their debut album, *The Gilded Palace of Sin,* in 1969. The project won Parsons many fans in the music community, including such heavyweights as the Rolling Stones. During this time Parsons forged a close friendship with Stones guitarist Keith Richards who introduced him to the excesses of the rock 'n' roll lifestyle. . . .

With a backing band that included Emmylou Harris, Parsons recorded [his first solo album] *G.P.* and released it in late 1972. After a small tour, the band reentered the studio to record the follow-up, *Grievous Angel*. A few weeks after the sessions were completed, Parsons . . . died of a drug and alcohol overdose on September 19, 1973. After the funeral, Parsons' body was stolen by his road manager who, in accordance with Parsons' wishes, took Parsons' body . . . to Joshua Tree [National Monument] and cremated it.

lorded over the album's final mix. All a singer really needed to bring to a session was his or her voice. And so it was really rather revolutionary when, instead of being told what to do and how to play, artists like Waylon Jennings, Bobby Bare, and Willie Nelson (each of them established and respected Nashville artists with hit songs dotting their resumes) decided it was high time they got to choose their own songs and play them their own way. On top of that, they insisted they should be allowed to use their road bands in the studio. Not that they didn't respect the technical prowess of the Nashville session men, it just seemed to make far greater sense to use pickers with whom they worked all year long on the road.[65]

While producers resisted the methods of the outlaws, fans could not get enough. In fact, the first country record to achieve platinum status (selling more than 1 million units) was *Wanted! The Outlaws,* a 1976 collaboration with Jennings, Nelson, Tompall Glaser, and Jessi Colter (Jennings's wife).

With a solid hit behind them, the renegade underground quickly became mainstream and dozens of songs brandishing the outlaw attitude appeared on records. Songs by various artists such as "Lonesome, On'ry and Mean," "Wasted Days and Wasted Nights," "Whiskey Bent and Hell Bound," "Here I Am Drunk Again," "Long-haired Redneck," and "Take This Job and Shove It" left little doubt as to the attitudes of the Nashville outlaws.

While artists such as Freddy Fender, Linda Hargrove, Mickey Newbury, Billy Joe Shaver, and Hank Williams Jr. rode the outlaw bandwagon, Jennings and Nelson were out front selling millions of records. Jennings used his rich baritone to sing about Willie and Waylon and the boys down in "Luckenbach, Texas." He also recorded duets with Nelson such as "Mammas Don't Let Your Babies Grow Up to Be Cowboys" that quickly became staples of '70s country—and even rock—radio. Meanwhile, Nelson's *Red Headed Stranger*—an album that shocked record executives for its sparse, acoustic arrangements—went platinum almost immediately upon its release.

Nelson's hippie-cowboy outfits, long hair, and beard, along with his well-known love for marijuana, did not amuse the Nashville establishment. While there was little they could do, considering the singer's success, there was a concerted effort in the 1980s to present a clean-cut, conservative image in areas where producers still maintained creative control.

Attracting New Audiences

While Nelson and Jennings remained extremely popular and influenced a generation of future country stars, the outlaw era faded in the late '70s. Nashville producers returned to their formulaic sound and began promoting squeaky-clean artists such as Debbie Boone, Tanya Tucker, Ronnie Milsap,

Willie Nelson's long hair and outlaw persona became a popular image for many country musicians in the 1970s.

Crystal Gayle, Lee Greenwood, and Janie Fricke. Songs such as Boone's excessively sentimental "You Light Up My Life" and Johnny Lee's over produced "Lookin' for Love" were an unabashed return to the 1960s countrypolitan style and were meant to appeal to a middle-aged, middle-class, conservative audience. In fact, the music became so pop-oriented that Boris Weintraub of the *Washington Star* wrote,

"Perhaps it is time to find a new term to replace 'country.' Because good or bad, there is precious little country left in today's country music."[66]

Not everyone fit into the middle-of-the-road formula bemoaned by Weintraub, however. When the band Alabama came along in the early 1980s, they returned the country sound to country music. And this group of cousins, who grew up on cotton farms

The Urban Cowboys

Country music made it to the silver screen in the 1980s, as movies such as Willie Nelson's *Honeysuckle Rose,* Dolly Parton's *Nine to Five,* and Loretta Lynn's *Coal Miner's Daughter* introduced mainstream America to the lives of country hit makers. But it was the movie *Urban Cowboy* that did the most to make country music and its culture an '80s fad. The film featured Hollywood sex symbol John Travolta, who had starred in the dance hit *Saturday Night Fever* only three years earlier. And when he traded his white disco suit for jeans and a cowboy hat, Travolta's *Urban Cowboy* became the country version of *Saturday Night Fever.*

The movie takes place in Gilley's, a Houston bar owned by country singer Mickey Gilley. Travolta plays Bud, a young farmer who recently moved to Houston to work on the oil rigs. The country soundtrack is provided by Gilley, Kenny Rogers, the Charlie Daniels Band, and others.

Urban Cowboy was hardly Oscar material, but the movie features line-dancing, mechanical bulls, and country fashions. These fads quickly spread across the United States in the '80s as country bars reminiscent of Gilley's opened everywhere from New York City to Akron, Ohio. Country record sales also jumped, helped in part by the movie's popularity. While country made up about 10 percent of the market in the late 1970s, by 1982 it had increased to 15 percent. Meanwhile, the number of country radio stations doubled from 1,050 to 2,100 between 1978 and 1982.

John Travolta in the 1980 hit movie Urban Cowboy.

The band Alabama *dominated the country music charts in the 1980s.*

near Fort Payne, Alabama, was one of the first bands to gain acceptance in a business that generally promoted individual singers.

With tight three-part harmonies, down-home fiddle licks, and anthemlike songs such as "Mountain Music," Alabama was propelled to superstardom, racking up twenty-one number one records between 1980 and 1987. In 1989 they were elected Artist of the Decade by the Academy of Country Music, and by the late 1990s, the band had doubled their tally of number one records. Having sold more than 60 million records total, the band ranks with Elvis Presley, the Beatles, and the Rolling Stones as one of the top-selling acts in history.

Alabama's appeal reached beyond the typical 1980s country listeners to a younger audience. As Wolff writes: "Gently blending pop and country into easily digestible formulas, their sound appeals across generations; they're just rebellious enough for the young folks, but their parents also dig the boys' pretty harmonies, sentimental soft spots, and old-fashioned family values."[67]

Alabama's popularity showed producers that youth-oriented bands could sell records, and a host of groups such as Sawyer Brown, Southern Pacific, the Desert Rose Band, and the Kentucky Headhunters were promoted throughout the '80s. Younger audiences were also attracted to the Judds, a singing mother-daughter group that combined mother Naomi's old-time country roots with daughter Wynonna's strong bluesy vocal style.

New Traditionalism

While superstar acts such as the Judds and Alabama dominated the charts in the second half of the '80s, a new crop of young musicians gained notice in Nashville. Singer-songwriters such as Lyle Lovett, Dwight Yoakam, Randy Travis, John Anderson, and George Strait produced debut albums that were well received, and all remained popular throughout the 1990s.

The music they played is categorized as "new traditionalism." There is an honesty in this style that represents the antithesis of the conventional overproduced, slick country music of the '80s. This return to a basic traditional country style is discussed on the Country Music Hall of Fame website:

[New (or "Neo") Traditionalism is a] stylistic throwback to a time when virtuosity and musical integrity were more important than image. [This style] looked to the elders of country music for inspiration and was a precursor to the more general categorization known as New Country.

[Starting in the 1980s] Ricky Skaggs, a picking prodigy who took his inspiration from [bluegrass founders] Bill Monroe and Ralph Stanley . . . went against the tenor

of the time and helped bring country back home to its roots.

The old was not only new again, it was a welcome relief. Skaggs was not alone, however. Artists like Randy Travis used a strong sense of melody and a carefully crafted vocal delivery to help bring New Traditionalism to the vanguard of country music.[68]

Proponents of new traditionalism covered a wide variety of styles, from Lovett's western swing to Yoakam's guitar-heavy Bakersfield Sound. Steve Earle's hot, outlaw-tinged songs brought hard-country, modern honky-tonk, and newgrass to a new generation of rock fans. As country star Mary Chapin Carpenter says: "Steve Earle really turned a lot of people on to country music who never, ever would have listened to it otherwise. . . . It had muscle and it had attitude and it had edge."[69]

Women in the New Tradition

Women such as Carpenter were among the group of female artists playing the new traditional style. Others included Nanci Griffith, who was discovered by Nashville producers playing folk music in Austin, Texas, and Kathy Mattea, who had a major hit with Griffith's "Love at the Five and Dime."

Two other women who played the new traditional style, Carlene Carter and Rosanne Cash, descended from "country royalty." Carlene Carter is the daughter of 1950s honky-tonk star Carl Smith and June Carter Cash, who herself is the daughter of Maybelle Carter of the pioneering country music Carter Family. Rosanne Cash is the child of Johnny Cash and his first wife, Vivian. (June Carter married Johnny Cash in 1965 after the girls were born.)

Carlene Carter mixed country, rock, swing, rockabilly, and honky-tonk on her 1990 breakthrough album *I Fell in Love*. Her sound was achieved with a cast of country and rock luminaries including guitarist James Burton, who

The country music style termed "new traditionalism" was marked by a return to honest, simple songs by artists such as Carlene Carter.

once backed Elvis; drummer Jim Keltner, who played with John Lennon after the Beatles broke up; and backup singer Nicolette Larson, who sang with Neil Young as well as recorded her own best-selling album.

Cash also experimented with various styles, playing real country on the album *Seven Year Ache,* then shocking Nashville—and many of her fans—by recording the new wave–tinged *Rhythm and Romance*. All the while, Cash remained high on the country charts with neotraditional singles such as "I Don't Know Why You Don't Want Me."

Of all the new traditionalists, k.d. lang may be the most unique. As one of the only vegetarian lesbians to top the charts in Nashville, she is described by Robert Oermann:

> Easily the kookiest of [the new traditionalists], lang had a wildly physical stage show, wore a spikey crew-cut hairdo, and dressed in "retro" square-dance skirts, embroidered cowgirl blouses, and cut-off western boots. But she also had a wallop of a voice and devoutly wished to be a reincarnation of Patsy Cline. Fans as well as Nashville industry loved her over-the-top performances, but radio shunned her records. [70]

Even without airplay, lang's loyal fans helped her albums *Shadowland* and *Absolute Torch and Twang* go gold, that is, sell more than half a million copies each.

Hats and Hunks

While the new traditionalists sold records in respectable numbers, it was the "new country" artists such as Garth Brooks, Shania Twain, Faith Hill, and LeAnn Rimes who did the most to promote country music in the 1990s.

New country relies on rich southern-accented vocals sung over a driving rock drumbeat and electric guitars. While fiddles and pedal steel guitars are often heard, orchestrated string sections, syrupy backup vocals, and songs picked by producers have been banished.

New country provided a visual, as well as musical, dimension with the growing popularity of country music television in the early '90s. And the videos produced by the young new country artists feature what Wolff describes as "hunks in hats, pretty gals in boots, and bright-eyed freshly scrubbed faces. . . . And who for goodness sake could take their eyes off that bellybutton on Shania Twain?"[71]

While traditionalists balked at new country's flash, few could argue with its astonishing financial success. Between 1989 and 1991 alone, country album sales doubled from $500 million to $1 billion. They doubled again by 1995, and by 1996 two out of every three albums on the country charts were declared gold, platinum, or multiplatinum. In 1994 seventy country artists achieved gold or platinum sales, compared with about ten a year in the 1980s.

Brooks and Twain

Oklahoma-born Garth Brooks led Nashville through this economic boom

Garth Brooks's showy style and upbeat sound propelled country music to new heights in the 1990s.

Country Music Patriotism

Country music has always been tinged with patriotism, and when terrorists flew airplanes into the World Trade Center Towers and the Pentagon on September 11, 2001, country artists responded almost immediately. Chris Dickinson writes about country's patriotism in the Los Angeles Times:

If there's any question that country music speaks to people in times of trouble, one need look no further than the telecast of the Country Music Assn. Awards a few weeks ago. For the first time in public, Alan Jackson performed a new song about the terrorist attacks of Sept. 11. "Did you shout out in anger in fear for your neighbor, or did you just sit down and cry?" he sang on "Where Were You (When the World Stopped Turning)?"

Although the song was not yet released on record, the emotional ballad hit an immediate nerve. Inundated by listener requests, radio stations began playing the audio portion of Jackson's song lifted from his live performance. Now stations are playing the album version, and the song resides in the upper reaches of the *Billboard* singles chart. . . . Jackson isn't the only country artist whose music has addressed Sept. 11. Recent patriotic songs have come from Aaron Tippin, Charlie Daniels and Randy Travis. Hank Williams Jr.'s upcoming CD, "The Almeria Club & Other Selected Venues," will include "America Will Survive," a reworking of his previous hit "A Country Boy Can Survive." In certain cases, songs recorded before Sept. 11 that contain a patriotic flavor have also gained an unexpected lift, including Lee Greenwood's early-'80s hit "God Bless the U.S.A." Brooks & Dunn's "Only in America" and David Ball's "Riding with Private Malone."

The plethora of patriotic country material comes as little surprise. Country music—with its straightforward emphasis on home, family, dislocation and heartache—has a long history of directly addressing hard times.

time. His 1991 album *Ropin' the Wind* debuted at number one on the pop and country charts—the first country album to do so. This album and his 1990 *No Fences* both sold over 10 million copies.

Brooks was more than a record executive's dream, however. With his down-home personality, Brooks put his family first and represented the humble and endearing values of country music. But when he strapped on his guitar and took to the stage, Brooks took his cues more from rocker Bruce Springsteen than from honky-tonker Hank Williams. He jumped, danced, strutted, swung from the rafters on cables, and occasionally smashed his guitar, all the while singing into his headset microphone. And his brand of hard-rocking country appealed to a wide audience of urban, suburban, and country folks, best demonstrated when Brooks attracted more than 200,000 people to New York City's Central Park for a free concert in 1997.

By drawing crowds nearly half as big as those at Woodstock, and by selling more than 66 million albums in the 1990s, Brooks changed the country music industry and opened the door for other new country acts such as Clint Black, Alan Jackson, and Vince Gill, all of whom had their roots in new traditionalism, but whose beat was closer to country rock.

Shania Twain was perhaps the most controversial of the new country artists, at least when she first arrived on the scene. Born in Ontario, Canada, Eileen Twain changed her name to Shania and quickly became the Madonna of country with her lively dance routines and provocative outfits. But Twain projected more than just a telegenic image—she had talent to spare.

Like Brooks, Twain's first two albums, *The Woman in Me* and *Come on Over,* sold an astounding 10 million copies each. (Twain was the first female artist to sell 10 million back-to-back albums.) Twain's producer (and husband), Robert John "Mutt" Lange,

Shania Twain's Canadian roots and penchant for skimpy outfits brought controversy to country music in the 1990s.

had previously worked with heavy metal bands such as Def Leppard and AC/DC, and both albums are influenced by new country, honky-tonk, rockabilly, and swing.

In the late '90s Brooks and Twain formed a golden country music triangle with the Dixie Chicks, who utilized the old-time bluegrass sound of fiddle, banjo, and guitar to shoot straight to the

The Dixie Chicks

The Dixie Chicks were one of the top-selling country acts of the late 1990s, and their neo-bluegrass sound has broad crossover appeal among both pop and country fans. Their band biography is posted on CountryStars.com:

There's old country. There's new country. Then there are the Dixie Chicks. Natalie Maines, Martie Seidel and Emily Robison have taken the Texas-bred sound of a fiddle, banjo, dobro and crystal-clear vocal harmonies into whole new territory. They are the rare act that comes along a few times in a generation that is destined to shake things up, rewrite the rules and become the new musical trendsetters.

The public has certainly noticed. The Dixie Chicks' first . . . album *Wide Open Spaces* has become the biggest selling album ever by a country duo or group—racking up some 6 million sales by the time their second album, *Fly,* was completed. The tremendous sales only demonstrates that while the Dixie Chicks have established themselves as a true country music act, they have also won over audiences outside the country genre. In a music field routinely known for selling to the conservative 30 and over crowd, more than 60% of the Dixie Chicks sales have been to consumers under the age of 25. Their concert audience is as likely to be comprised of entire rows of young women in their early teens and twenties as it is to include middle age couples and entire families complete with pre-teen girls dressed like their musical idols and singing every Dixie Chicks' song word for word. . . .

For years, the Texas-trio booked their own dates, hired equipment and carted it to and from gigs themselves. Originally performing on a street corner in Dallas, the band's combination of bluegrass, cowgirl music and western swing earned them $300 in their very first hour and soon led them to barbecue joints, corporate gigs . . . and regional nightclubs.

The Dixie Chicks performing at the 1999 Country Music Awards.

top of the charts with their 1998 *Wide Open Spaces,* which quickly sold 6 million copies. Their attractive and clever videos are some of the favorites on country music TV, and their independent attitudes have influenced a new generation of female country fans.

Twenty-First-Century Country

Although the country music business experienced slowing sales in the recession of 2001, dozens of hot young country artists continued to fill the airwaves with music influenced by everything from Bill Monroe to 'NSync. In videos such as Toby Keith's "I Wanna Talk About Me," the singer looks more like Kid Rock than Johnny Cash, and the rapid-fire verses recited by Keith might be classified as country rap.

Country has always embraced diverse musical forms, from blues and jazz in the 1930s to rock and roll in the '60s. This trend continues in the twenty-first century. An album by a modern best-selling country artist may contain a honky-tonk song, a bluegrass breakdown, a few country rockers, some western swing, and even a Caribbean-flavored number. Unlike earlier decades, there are few rules in modern country except to sing from the heart, tell a good story, and let the audience kick up their heels and dance.

• Notes •

Chapter One: The Early Years of Country

1. Quoted in Patrick Carr, ed., *The Illustrated History of Country Music.* Garden City, NY: Doubleday, 1979, p. 1.
2. Steven D. Price, *Old as the Hills.* New York: Viking Press, 1975, p. 9.
3. Quoted in Carr, *The Illustrated History of Country Music,* p. 3.
4. Price, *Old as the Hills,* p. 9.
5. Quoted in Carr, *The Illustrated History of Country Music,* p. 4.
6. Quoted in Carr, *The Illustrated History of Country Music,* p. 9.
7. Quoted in Robert K. Oermann, *A Century of Country.* New York: TV Books, 1999, p. 11.
8. Quoted in Robert K. Oermann, *America's Music: The Roots of Country.* Atlanta: Turner Publishing, 1996, pp. 12–13.
9. Quoted in Carr, *The Illustrated History of Country Music,* p. 26.
10. Quoted in Oermann, *A Century of Country,* p. 18.
11. Quoted in Oermann, *A Century of Country,* p. 11.
12. Quoted in Oermann, *America's Music,* p. 37.
13. Quoted in Roy Acuff and William Neely, *Roy Acuff's Nashville.* New York: Perigree Books, 1983, pp. 78–79.
14. Quoted in Oermann, *America's Music,* p. 40.

Chapter Two: The Sounds of Bluegrass

15. Quoted in Tom Ewing, ed., *The Bill Monroe Reader.* Chicago: University of Illinois Press, 2000, pp. 11, 31.
16. Quoted in Oermann, *A Century of Country,* p. 80.
17. Quoted in Robert Cantwell, *Bluegrass Breakdown.* New York: De Capo Press, 1992, p. 68.
18. Bob Artis, *Bluegrass.* New York: Hawthorn Books, 1975, p. 25.
19. Price, *Old as the Hills,* p. 50.
20. Oermann, *A Century of Country,* p. 85.
21. Artis, *Bluegrass,* p. 33.
22. Quoted in Oermann, *A Century of Country,* p. 87.
23. Art Howard, "New Take on an Old Form: Souped-up Bluegrass Puts Its Stamp on Rock," September 29, 2001. www.voyagermagazine.com.
24. Quoted in Howard, "New Take on an Old Form."
25. Quoted in Ewing, *The Bill Monroe Reader,* p. 179.

Chapter Three: Honky-Tonk Music

26. Country Music Foundation, *Country: The Music and Musicians.* New York: Abbeville Press, 1994, p. 153.

27. Quoted in Country Music Foundation, *Country,* p. 155.
28. Quoted in Country Music Foundation, *Country,* p. 161.
29. Bruce Honick, "1940s: We'll Go Honky-Tonkin'," 2000–1. www.country weekly.com.
30. Kurt Wolff, *Country Music: The Rough Guide.* London: Rough Guides, 2000, p. 109.
31. Wolff, *Country Music,* pp. 158–59.
32. Quoted in Country Music Foundation, *Country,* p. 172.
33. Wolff, *Country Music,* p. 157.
34. Quoted in Nicholas Dawidoff, *In the Country of Country.* New York: Pantheon Books, 1997, p. 64.
35. Quoted in Dawidoff, *In the Country of Country,* p. 64.
36. Quoted in Country Music Foundation, *Country,* p. 226.

Chapter Four: Cowboy Music and Western Swing

37. Bill C. Malone, *Country Music, U.S.A.* Austin, TX: American Folklore Society, 1968, p. 149.
38. Quoted in Malone, *Country Music, U.S.A.,* p. 153.
39. Malone, *Country Music, U.S.A.,* pp. 153–54.
40. Wolff, *Country Music,* p. 94.
41. Quoted in Cary Ginell and Roy Lee Brown, *Milton Brown and the Founding of Western Swing.* Chicago: University of Illinois Press, 1994, p. 63.
42. Quoted in Ginell and Brown, *Milton Brown,* p. 109.
43. Wolff, *Country Music,* p. 76.

Chapter Five: Rockabilly Music

44. Wolff, *Country Music,* p. 259.
45. "Wynonie Harris, n.d." www.hoyhoy.com.
46. Oermann, *A Century of Country,* p. 136.
47. Craig Morrison, *Go Cat Go!* Chicago: University of Illinois Press, 1996, p. 36.
48. Quoted in Country Music Foundation, *Country,* p. 193.
49. Quoted in Oermann, *A Century of Country,* p. 136.
50. Quoted in Oermann, *A Century of Country,* p. 136.
51. Quoted in Oermann, *A Century of Country,* p. 142.
52. Quoted in Oermann, *A Century of Country,* p. 146.

Chapter Six: The Nashville Hit Makers

53. Quoted in Oermann, *A Century of Country,* p. 154.
54. Quoted in Joli Jensen, *Nashville Sound: Authenticity, Commercialization, and Country Music.* Nashville: Vanderbilt University Press, 1998, p. 77.
55. Quoted in Malone, *Country Music, U.S.A.,* p. 253.
56. Wolff, *Country Music,* p. 287.
57. Quoted in Wolff, *Country Music,* p. 322.
58. Wolff, *Country Music,* p. 315.
59. Wolff, *Country Music,* p. 311.
60. Quoted in Eric W. Penman, "Roger Miller: King of the Road," 2000. home.nycap.rr.com.

61. Wolff, *Country Music,* p. 312.
62. Malone, *Country Music, U.S.A.,* p. 259.

Chapter Seven: New Sounds, New Fans

63. Quoted in Oermann, *America's Music,* p. 201.
64. "Gram Parsons, n.d.," www.tela link.net.
65. Wolff, *Country Music,* p. 338.

66. Quoted in Wolff, *Country Music,* p. 424.
67. Wolff, *Country Music,* p. 428.
68. Country.com, "Country Music Genres," 2001. www.halloffame. org.
69. Quoted in Oermann, *A Century of Country,* p. 294.
70. Oermann, *A Century of Country,* p. 294.
71. Wolff, *Country Music,* p. 502.

• For Further Reading •

Country Music Foundation, *Country: The Music and Musicians*. New York: Abbeville Press, 1994. The story of country music from its nineteenth-century roots to the 1990s written by a who's who of well-known music journalists including Chet Flippo, Robert Palmer, and Nick Tosches. Published by the entity that runs the Country Music Hall of Fame & Museum.

Editors of Time-Life Books, *Classic Country: The Golden Age of Country Music: The 20's Through the 70's*. San Diego: Time-Life Books, 2001. More than three hundred photos and well-written biographies on more than fifty artists, including the Carter Family, Roy Acuff, Ernest Tubb, Bill Monroe, Jimmie Rodgers, Loretta Lynn, Johnny Cash, Merle Haggard, and Willie Nelson.

D.L. Gish, *Country Music*. North Mankato, MN: Smart Apple Media, 2001. Traces the history of country music while describing musical instruments, performers, and styles such as bluegrass, honky-tonk, and country rock.

Robert K. Oermann, *America's Music: The Roots of Country*. Atlanta: Turner Publishing, 1996. The history of country music as told through quotes from its biggest stars past and present, such as Bill Monroe, Dolly Parton, Willie Nelson, Garth Brooks, Alan Jackson, the Judds, and dozens of others. Taken from the Nashville Network's thirteen-part documentary on country music.

Jack L. Roberts, *Garth Brooks*. San Diego: Lucent Books, 2000. A fascinating biography that follows this musician's rise from obscurity to world fame.

Robert Santelli, Holly George-Warren, and Jim Brown, eds., *American Roots Music*. New York: Henry N. Abrams, 2001. A companion text to a four-part PBS series of the same name, with easy-to-read chapters on early country, blues, bluegrass, Cajun, gospel, and more.

• Works Consulted •

Books and Periodicals

Roy Acuff and William Neely, *Roy Acuff's Nashville.* New York: Perigree Books, 1983. The autobiography of *Grand Ole Opry* star Roy Acuff, "the King of Country Music."

Bob Artis, *Bluegrass.* New York: Hawthorn Books, 1975. The famous pickers and singers who delivered that hammering, driving string-band sound from the early days of Bill Monroe to the "newgrass revival" of the 1970s.

Mary A. Bufwack and Robert K. Oermann, *Finding Her Voice: The Saga of Women in Country Music.* New York: Crown Publishers, 1993. The stories of the Carter Family, Dolly Parton, Reba McEntire, and dozens of other women who have been influential in country.

Robert Cantwell, *Bluegrass Breakdown.* New York: De Capo Press, 1992. An in-depth reading of bluegrass music, including its musical, social, and cultural aspects.

Patrick Carr, ed., *The Illustrated History of Country Music.* Garden City, NY: Doubleday, 1979. The story of country music embellished with dozens of great photos, published by the editors of *Country Music* magazine.

Nicholas Dawidoff, *In the Country of Country.* New York: Pantheon Books, 1997. A journey across America to the rural highways, tiny towns, poor valleys, and railroad sidings, where the sounds of country music—and many of its most famous stars—were born.

Chris Dickinson, "Response to Sept. 11 a Natural for Country Singers," *Los Angeles Times,* December 19, 2001. An article about Alan Jackson's song "Where Were You (When the World Stopped Turning)?" and the impact of country music during times of national tragedy.

Tom Ewing, ed., *The Bill Monroe Reader.* Chicago: University of Illinois Press, 2000. Several dozen short articles about the father of bluegrass music written by musicians, scholars, critics, and others.

Cary Ginell and Roy Lee Brown, *Milton Brown and the Founding of Western Swing.* Chicago: University of Illinois Press, 1994. The early history of western swing as recalled in narratives by musicians and eyewitnesses who saw Brown's band perform during their short-lived heyday in the early 1930s.

Joli Jensen, *Nashville Sound: Authenticity, Commercialization, and Country Music.* Nashville: Vanderbilt University Press, 1998. Attitudes about money, fame, ego, and music intersect in this book about the country sounds of Nashville.

Bill C. Malone, *Country Music, U.S.A.* Austin: American Folklore Society, 1968. The social and musical history of American country music written by a history professor.

Craig Morrison, *Go Cat Go!* Chicago: University of Illinois Press, 1996. The history of rockabilly from its early '50s roots to the revival in recent times.

Robert K. Oermann, *A Century of Country.* New York: TV Books, 1999. The richly illustrated story of the people who made country music what it is today, based on the Nashville Network's thirteen-part documentary series.

Steven D. Price, *Old as the Hills.* New York: Viking Press, 1975. The story of bluegrass music from its eighteenth-century roots to the modern revival.

Kurt Wolff, *Country Music: The Rough Guide.* London: Rough Guides, 2000. An exhaustive handbook to American country music with in-depth biographies of stars, essays on history, album reviews, and more than 250 pictures.

Internet Sources

Damien Allen, "Charlie [sic] Pride—First African American Inducted into the Country Music Hall of Fame," 2001. www.topblacks.com. A site dedicated to one of the best-selling African American country singers in history.

Country.com, "Country Music Genres," 2001. www.halloffame.org. A site maintained by the Country Music Hall of Fame that defines more than a dozen styles of country music from bluegrass to alternative.

Bill Dahl, "Wynonie Harris Biography," 2001. www.rollingstone.com. A biography of blues shouter Wynonie Harris, whose musical style inspired countless rockabilly and rock-and-roll artists.

"Gram Parsons," n.d. www.telalink.net. A short biography of a man who, in less than ten years, influenced a generation of country rock musicians.

Joe Hauler, "Gram Parsons Biography," 2001. www.rollingstone.com. A detailed biography of Gram Parsons, his life, his work, and his influence on country rock music.

Heritage Music Review, "A Corn Licker Still in Georgia by Gid Tanner & His Skillet Lickers," n.d. www.voyager records.com. A review of the recent reissue on CD of the classic Skillet Lickers skit that sold millions of records in 1927 and was performed hundreds of times on radio *Barn Dance* shows.

Bruce Honick, "1940s: We'll Go Honky-Tonkin'," 2000–1. www.country weekly.com. An article about honky-tonk music during the World War II era from the online version of *Country Weekly,* a magazine catering to the country music industry and fans.

Art Howard, "New Take on an Old Form: Souped-up Bluegrass Puts Its Stamp on Rock," September 29, 2001. www.voyagermagazine.com. An article about the band Leftover Salmon and how they were influenced by bluegrass and newgrass music.

Jones Media Network, "The Dixie Chicks," 1995–2001. www.country stars.com. A site with information about country music's hottest stars, the Dixie Chicks.

James Ward Lee, "Texas My Texas," 2000. www.virtualtexan.com. A website with excerpts about the history of honky-tonks from Lee's book *Texas My Texas.*

"Leon McAuliffe—Western Swing's Most Famous Steel Guitarist," n.d. www.well.com. A site dedicated to the man who is considered one of the world's greatest steel guitar players.

"A Little About Hee Haw," n.d. http://bushresearch.com. A site dedicated to the country music/comedy television show that aired for twenty-five years.

Eric W. Penman, "Roger Miller: King of the Road," 2000. home.nycap.rr. com. A site dedicated to the man who wrote "Dang Me," "King of the Road," "You Can't Rollerskate in a Buffalo Herd," and other 1960s country wonders.

RollingStone.com, "Jimmie Rodgers Biography," 2001.www.rollingstone. com. The *Rolling Stone* story of the man who is considered the founder of country music.

Earl Scruggs, "Biography of Earl Scruggs," n.d. http://flattscruggs.top cities.com/earlbio.html. The life and times of Earl Scruggs, considered by many to be the world's greatest banjo picker.

Mike Seeger, "An Historical and Musical Background on the Southern Appalachian Region," n.d. www.mike seeger.pair.com/html/2_hist.html. An article about the roots of country music by a founding member of the renown 1960s folk group New Lost City Ramblers.

"Wynonie Harris," n.d. www.hoyhoy. com. A site with pictures, biographical information, and great sound-clip links dedicated to the man who started the rock revolution with "Good Rockin' Tonight."

• Index •

• Picture Credits •

• About the Author •

Stuart A. Kallen is the author of more than 150 nonfiction books for children and young adults. He has written on topics ranging from the theory of relativity to rock-and-roll history to life on the American frontier. In addition, Mr. Kallen has written award-winning children's videos and television scripts. In his spare time he is a singer/songwriter/guitarist in San Diego, California.